First published in 2005 by
CURRACH PRESS
55A Spruce Avenue, Stillorgan Industrial Park, Blackrock, Co. Dublin

www.currach.ie

1 3 5 4 2

Cover by Liam Furlong
Front cover picture by Charles P. Friel
Back cover picture by Barry Carse
Maps by Joe Jennings
Origination by Currach Press
Printed by Betaprint Ltd, Dublin

The author has asserted his moral rights.

ISBN 1-85607-925-2

Acknowledgements
The author and publisher gratefully acknowledge the permission of the following
to use photographic material in their copyright:
Belfast Telegraph: 247; The Father Browne SJ Collection: pp. 164 (Refs. top – 11-
80-7 and bottom – 11-79-3) and p.167 (Ref. 11-79-34); Barry Carse: 191, 192,
194, 196, 201, 206, 209 and 224; R. M. Casserley: 57 and 180; L. Daly
Collection: 133; *Donegal Annual:* 155; Oliver Doyle: 214 and 229; Charles P. Friel:
pp.171, 217, 218 and 220; *Irish Examiner:* 60, 76, 158 and 199; Irish Railway
Record Society: frontispiece, 16, 18, 34, 55, 63, 79, 80, 82, 89, 94, 97, 102, 111,
112, 114, 115, 118, 120, 121, 125, 127 (bottom), 131, 143, 148, 154, 160, 176,
177, 185, 216, 226 and 242; *The Irish Times:* 202 and 231; National Library of
Ireland: pp.29 (Ref. E592), 32 (Ref. R 8413), 78 (Ref. R 7626), 110 (Ref. O'Dea
33/80), 127 (top – Ref. CAB 5638), 152 (Ref. R 9339) and 187 (Ref MOR 1997);
M. A. Keating: p.182 (both); Seán Kennedy: pp.67, 82, 86, 90, 136, 137, 138,
142, 144, 145, 245 and 249 (top); Walter McGrath: 58 and 157; G. Morrison:
p.132; David Murray: 162; Ivo Peters: 141; Public Record Office of Northern
Ireland (PRONI): 40; Paul Quinlan: 107; Sligo County Library: 129; Joe Taylor:
p.62; National Museums & Galleries of Northern Ireland, Ulster Folk and
Transport Museum: pp.36 (Ref. WAG 3477) and 173 (Ref. L4124-9); Ulster
Museum: pp.23 (Ref. W10/46/1), 27 (Ref. W10/46/20) and 72 (Ref. W48/01/42).

Every effort has been made to trace copyright holders. If we have inadvertently
used copyright material without permission we apologise and will put it right in
future editions.

CONTENTS

Do mo thriúr mac: Conall, Rónán agus Alastar Mac Aongusa,
a mhol bun-smaoineamh an leabhair agus a thug an tacaíocht agus
an spreagadh cuí dom chun é a chur i dtoll a chéile.

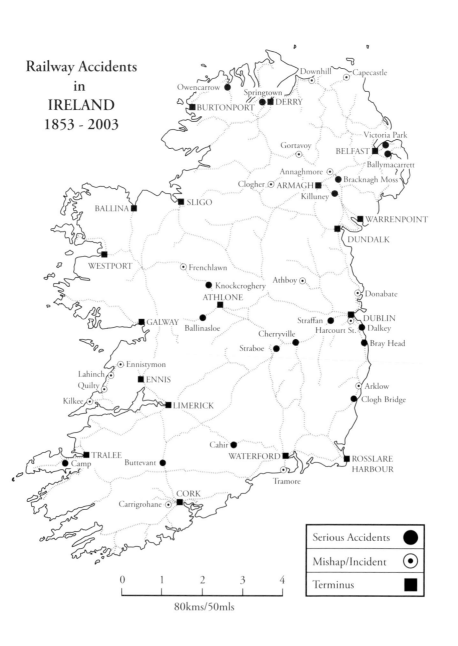

Railway Accidents
in
IRELAND
1853 - 2003

Owencarrow
Springtown
BURTONPORT   DERRY
Downhill   Capecastle
Victoria Park
Gortavoy   BELFAST
Annaghmore   Ballymacarrett
Clogher   ARMAGH   Bracknagh Moss
Killuney
BALLINA   SLIGO   WARRENPOINT
DUNDALK
WESTPORT   Frenchlawn   Athboy   Donabate
Knockcroghery
ATHLONE
GALWAY   Straffan   DUBLIN
Ballinasloe   Harcourt St.   Dalkey
Cherryville   Bray Head
Straboe
Ennistymon
Lahinch   ENNIS
Quilty   Arklow
Kilkee   LIMERICK   Clogh Bridge
Cahir
TRALEE   Camp   Buttevant   WATERFORD   ROSSLARE
HARBOUR
Tramore
CORK
Carrigrohane

Serious Accidents   ●
Mishap/Incident   ⊙
Terminus   ■

0   1   2   3   4
80kms/50mls

BUÍOCHAS

This book, written to inform and entertain rather than to extend railway research, has been in preparation for almost two years. It could never have been written in so short a time without the support of research carried out by many previous writers in the field of Irish railway history. Their published papers, pamphlets and books over the past century-and-a-half provided a considerable store of knowledge from which I have liberally drawn the stories and adventures featured in this volume.

I am greatly indebted to the library and archives of the Irish Railway Record Society at Heuston Station Dublin, especially to the Honorary Librarian, Tim Moriarty, and the Honorary Archivist, Brendan Pender, both of whom facilitated me with efficiency and courtesy. A wide circle of society members guided me to little-known railway mishaps that yielded fascinating stories when further researched and many members also went to considerable trouble on my behalf in seeking rare photographs to illustrate the destruction caused by specific crashes and mishaps. In particular, I wish to thank most sincerely Charles P. Friel, Seán Kennedy and Barry Carse for searching out and providing me with some photos of exceptional interest.

The meticulous research undertaken over many years by the editor of the *Journal of the Irish Railway Record Society*, the late Kevin A. Murray and his successor as editor, David Murray, provided a template for much of my own research. I also gratefully acknowledge the researches of the late Dr George Hadden of Wexford, the late Dr Edward Patterson of Belfast, Walter McGrath of Cork and John O'Meara of Dublin, all of whom contributed papers to the *Journal* during the past fifty years. Others from whose research I have drawn material are listed in the Select Bibliography at the back of the volume.

My warmest thanks to all who helped me in the compilation of this book. *Nár laga sibh!*

Brian Mac Aongusa
Deireadh Fómhair 2005

PREFACE

Railway accidents have had a strange fascination for many people for generations. No matter how slight the damage caused or how few casualties are involved, the very fact that a train leaves the railway tracks and ploughs ahead uncontrolled by any guiding rails, fills the imagination with awe and wonder. Sensational headlines appear and people want to know what awful consequences followed, how much worse the accident could have been and, more importantly, why it happened in the first place. Frequently human frailty is the cause but, as revealed in this book, there are often less obvious reasons. Fatigue, intrigue, overwork, carelessness, stubborn animals, the elements or even the longings of the heart have caused accidents on the railways of Ireland.

The selection of crashes and mishaps featured in this book provides a unique insight not only to railway working in Ireland over the past century-and-a-half, but also to the fortitude and ingenuity of Irish people when confronted with unexpected difficulties. The accidents described in the following pages include the great railway tragedies that happened at Armagh, Camp, Cahir and Buttevant, as well as politically-inspired mishaps of the Civil War period and of more recent times in South Armagh and County Louth including the episode that became known as The Sallins Mail Train Robbery. 'Acts of God' such as the Owencarrow Viaduct disaster in Donegal are included with other lesser-known incidents caused by wind, snow, goats, a steam-roller or a love tryst. All have one common feature in that the trains involved came to a sudden and unexpected stop and this led to stories that make for interesting and often fascinating reading.

It is worth noting that the majority of accidents described in this book happened in the earlier rather than in the later part of the past 150 years. It is not generally realised that the number of railway accidents in Ireland has shown a marked decline over the past fifty years, largely due to the increasing sophistication and reliability of modern trains, tracks, signalling and locomotion technology. That no lives of fare-paying passengers have been lost while travelling on trains in Ireland for over twenty years is a substantial achievement of which both Iarnród Éireann (IÉ) and Northern Ireland Railways (NIR) can justly be proud. It highlights the superior safety of rail travel in Ireland compared with travel by road and points to the considerable efforts of railway staff throughout the country to ensure that travel by train is the safest of all.

Inquest and Inquiry

At the Coroner's Inquest held in Bray on 13 August a verdict was returned of 'accidental death resulting from the train crash at Bray Head'. But the following day Colonel W. Yolland opened a Board of Trade Inquiry to carry out an independent investigation of the accident and he arrived at a totally different conclusion. His report of 20 August revealed that a visit to the scene of the accident produced evidence that the engine was derailed by the uneven state of the track, which consisted of three different types of rail, both old and new. The joints between the rails were weak and poorly supported, without any guard-rail. The sleepers under the rails were rotten and a repair gang working on the line the evening before the accident had left the track in its bad condition.

Early on the morning of the accident the Permanent Way Inspector, William Cosgrave, with the Length-Ganger Simon Carty and the party of platelayers, had examined the line with a hand lamp and had found a low joint in the track on the bridge. The Inspector ordered some raising and lowering of the joints to be made, and the gauge adjusted here and there 'to make the road right'. Then, unknown to any superior, the Inspector went off in one direction and the Length-Ganger in the other direction, leaving the workmen to carry out the orders given to them. This was apparently done so that both men would able to say, should any mishap occur around Bray Head, that they had not altered the track. Colonel Yolland was highly critical of their behaviour and concluded that if these facts had been known at the Coroner's Inquest, there might not have been any verdict of accidental death. He added that the Inspector and the Length-Ganger were 'not proper men to be entrusted with looking after and relaying permanent way'.

The directors of the Dublin Wicklow & Wexford Railway were critical of several points made by Colonel Yolland in his report, but agreed generally with his conclusions. They thought that credit should have been given for the amount of new materials used on the railway and hotly denied that irregularity of the gauge or decay of the timbers were a factor in the accident. Colonel Yolland responded that he would not withdraw any of his remarks saying that 'a complete renewal of such a poorly-laid section was paramount, as the permanent way was in a very bad state'. Permanent Way Inspector Cosgrave and Length-Ganger Carty were blamed for their conduct and were dismissed by the company.

BALLYMACARRETT ACCIDENT COVER-UP

One of the earliest known photographs of the aftermath of a railway accident in Ireland featured the disaster at Ballymacarrett/*Baile Mhic Gearóid* in East Belfast on 13 May 1871 when a crowded evening train from County Down collided with a derailed engine causing the death of two passengers and injuries to over fifty. The accident was extraordinary in a number of respects. Among the injured was Mr W. R. Anketell, Chairman of the Belfast & County Down Railway and this fact would appear to have had a significant influence on the course of subsequent developments and investigations. Paramount to Mr Anketell was the protection of the interests of his company and he went to great lengths to ensure he would achieve that objective with total disregard for the interests of individual staff involved.

On the day following the crash the Belfast & County Down Railway issued the following announcement to the local press:

Sir,

I regret to have to inform you that a serious accident happened to the last up-train last night a short distance from Belfast Station, whereby two persons are known to have been killed and others seriously injured.

It appears to have been caused by the misconduct of a fireman who, as far as we know at present, wilfully ran his engine out of the station yard on to the main line as the up-train was approaching, whereby a serious collision was caused and a portion of the passenger train upset down the embankment.

The fireman was taken into custody within an hour after the occurrence and when arrested was found to be in a state of intoxication.

I am, Sir, your obedient servant,

T. C. Haines, general manager.

This extraordinarily tendentious statement was to set the tone and course of subsequent investigations into the cause of the Ballymacarrett accident.

Duties of the Staff

To try to understand the underlying causes of this accident, it is necessary to outline the duties undertaken by certain key staff on the day in question, as revealed at the inquiry. Driver Thomas Spence had been thirteen years in the service of the Belfast & County Down Railway (B&CDR) and three years as a driver. In the late afternoon of 13 May 1871 he returned to duty, but his fireman, Thomas Trainor, had preceded him to the shed at 4 p.m. to light the fire in the steam engine and prepare it for work. The engine was B&CDR 2-4-0 saddle-tank No 5, designed as a mixed-traffic engine that could work everything from goods trains to passenger expresses. When Thomas Spence reached the engine shed at 6 p.m., his fireman, Thomas Trainor, had raised steam, taken No 5 to the departure platform and hooked on to the 6.30 p.m. local train to Knock. Both men duly worked the train to Knock and arrived back in Belfast around 6.50 p.m. They put the empty carriages in a siding and Thomas Trainor then went for his supper at 7 p.m.

Driver Spence remained in the engine and with Samuel Eccles, the guard, proceeded to the goods yard to collect empty wagons for the night goods train, which was No 5's next duty. This task was completed by 7.25 p.m. and, as the loaded wagons were not yet ready, the driver left No 5 unattended and he too went for some refreshment, being joined by the foreman of the cleaners from the shed. On their way out from the yard, they met Fireman Trainor returning from his meal and took him with them to King's Pub in Ballymacarrett 'for a half-one of rum'. When Driver Spence was questioned at the inquest as to the amount of drink consumed, he was somewhat vague, but he and his fireman were reported to be sober when they returned to their engine at 8 p.m.

Their task now was to complete the make-up of the goods train. Following some shunting, it was necessary for their engine to take water and they moved to the water column at the end of the departure platform. Leaving his fireman alone on the footplate, Driver Spence climbed on to the saddle-tank, opened the manhole and inserted the water-bag swung over to him by a porter who turned on the supply. When the tank was full, the driver returned to the footplate to find that Fireman Trainor had somehow broken the handle of the steam injector, a vital part in the control of a steam engine. Some hard words were said, but at the subsequent trial Driver Spence denied suggestions by defence counsel that he had struck his fireman on the head. The engine continued the shunting with, according to the evidence, the engine handbrake screwed down and the regulator shut to compensate for the lack of control over the steam injector. The driver then left Fireman Trainor in charge of No 5, while he went off to get a substitute for the broken handle from the workshops at the far end of the yard from the terminus.

The Accident

Coming back from the workshops, Driver Spence was surprised to see his train moving away and then observing No 5 and her wagons coming to an abrupt halt some distance down the line. He immediately realised that something was wrong and began to run after the train. About 300 yards from the workshops he met Fireman Trainor running towards him saying that he was going to tell the shed foreman that No 5 had come off the rails. But both men knew that an up train was due at 8.25 p.m., so that their first duty should have been to run in the opposite direction in an attempt to wave that train to a stop. This thought occurred to the driver and he then continued down the line towards his engine only to see the collision happen before his eyes. Before he could reach No 5, he witnessed it being driven back and overturned with the leading carriages 'tumbled over the body'.

The up passenger train that evening consisted of ten vehicles from Donaghadee and Downparrick that were well-filled with excursionists returning from a day trip to Portpatrick in Scotland and with trippers who had been at Newtownards fair. Among the passengers was the Chairman of the B&CDR Board of Directors Mr W. R. Anketell. It was 8.20 p.m. on a fine evening with a slight fog in the air, as the train was on the stone bridge over Connswater coasting down the 1:100 bank towards Belfast, when the crew first saw the smoke of No 5 in the distance.

At first they took it for the exhaust of an engine on another train travelling east towards Hollywood, but as their train rounded the curve it became clear that No 5 was lying across the main line. Driver Robert Lyons immediately whistled for the brakes to be applied by the guards, flung his engine into reverse and opened the regulator, while Fireman George Green screwed down the tender brake and the guards wrestled with their handbrakes. By their combined efforts the train's speed was approximately halved to about 10 mph at the moment of impact, but the collision was a drastic one. No 5 was driven back about three rail lengths and finished up on its side down the embankment, bringing one of the wagons with it. The engine of the train returning to Belfast was thrown off the track and overturned, its leading end down the bank. The leading carriages of the train suffered severely. The front van disintegrated into splinters, over-ridden by the following carriage which was torn in half and had its buffer-rods driven into the engine's coal tender. The remaining carriages were thrown to one side, with the ends of the leading coaches driven in by the force of the impact.

Wreckage below the railway line at Ballymacarrett following the accident, 1871.

With such extensive damage it was amazing that only two people were killed in the crash – Ellen Bailey, a thirteen-year-old girl from Knock and John Craig, a student of Queen's College Belfast. Five other passengers were seriously injured and a further forty-six 'complained of being injured'. Driver Lyons and Fireman Green had jumped from the engine before impact and escaped with less serious injuries. Fireman Green's first action, like that of Driver Spence with his No 5, was to put the engine's fire out. Guard Wilson travelling in the leading van 'stuck to his post to the last' and had to be cut free from the wreckage. Although having only a scalp wound, he was badly shaken and his health never fully recovered.

Immediate Arrest

Retaliatory action by Mr W. R.Anketell was swift. He ordered the immediate arrest of Thomas Trainor, the fireman of No 5. When the collision occurred, Fireman Trainor was on his way to warn the engine shed foreman of No 5's derailment, but according to evidence he 'turned aside and left the premises altogether'. Clearly he passed the rest of the evening effacing the memory of his lapse in a tavern. He was found by the police 'drunk and asleep' in bed at his home after 10 p.m. that night. They arrested him and attested that he seemed unconscious of what had taken place. On his way to the police station he was 'continually enquiring what was wrong'.

When Thomas Trainor found himself before the Coroner's Inquest two days later, Mr W. R. Anketell was one of the Justices of the Peace on the bench. Not surprisingly, the jury returned a verdict:

> That Thomas Trainor did on the 13th day of May 1871 feloniously kill
> and slay one John Moore Craig, against the peace of our Sovereign Lady
> the Queen, her crown and dignity, and that he did at the same time kill
> and slay one Ellen Bailey…

As a consequence, Thomas Trainor was returned for trial on a charge of manslaughter.

Board of Trade Inquiry

In the meantime the Board of Trade appointed Colonel Rich to conduct the usual formal investigation into the cause of the accident. He forwarded his report to the directors of the B&CDR on 23 June 1871, causing some unease among that august body. Colonel Rich had somewhat alarmingly confined his strictures to the loose discipline that then prevailed at the Belfast terminus. He pointed out that the foreman of the cleaners, instead of drinking with the men, should have reported their misconduct. Proper supervision would have checked such irregularities as the fireman rather than the driver bringing the engine down to the platform and would have prevented the enginemen from going away together to drink, leaving the engine unattended. With regard to the accident itself, Colonel Rich placed all the blame on Fireman Trainor:

> The accident was, no doubt, caused by this man being so drunk as to be
> incapable of knowing what he was doing when he was left in charge of
> the engine on the siding by the workshops.

This may well be considered a strange conclusion from a member of so impartial a body as Her Majesty's Inspecting Officers of Railways. It was particularly strange when one considers that Thomas Trainor had not yet been tried on the charge of manslaughter brought against him following the Coroner's Inquest. In truth, Colonel Rich's comments and conclusion as to the intoxicated state of Thomas Trainor were *sub judice*.

Criminal Trial

A month later in July 1871 Thomas Trainor was tried, not in Co Down where the accident happened, but in Co Antrim. There he appeared before Judge Lawson, who had been Mr Anketell's tutor at Trinity College in Dublin. Thomas Trainor was found guilty and was sentenced to one year's hard labour. He was only 24-years-of-age and had been married for only three months. He had been with the B&CDR for over eleven years and had been a fireman since 1865. The Locomotive Superintendent, C. K. Domville, had thought highly of him and his prospects of promotion were good. Had he been tried in this present age, there would have been medical evidence, or a plea to consider human frailty, to help his defence. But the Victorian age was a harsh time, labour was cheap and the interests of the company and its shareholders had to be protected at all costs.

Cover-up

In reading the reports and documents concerning the Ballymacarrett accident of 1871, one cannot escape the conclusion that Mr W. R. Aketell, Chairman of the B&CDR, moved swiftly after the collision to arrange that blame would firmly be placed on one individual, rather than on the company's management. It is very clear that a drink culture was pervasive among staff at the Belfast terminus and that management control and supervision in this regard was loose and negligent. Mr Anketell must have been aware of this culture and was determined that it should not be publicly revealed. Had it been fully exposed, as was threatened in Colonel Rich's investigations, management negligence would properly have been identified as the root cause of the horrendous accident. The company consequently would have had to face serious accusations, as well as heavy claims for compensation.

The relationships that Mr Anketell had developed made it possible for him to protect the interests of the B&CDR and ensure that blame for the accident was clearly placed from the outset on one person, who may have been well-regarded but was lowly and dispensable. The B&CDR management and shareholders, rather than the staff, were unashamedly protected by Mr Acketell to a point where drink was hardly an issue when the dust had settled.

DRINK CULTURE AND THE RAILWAYS

Drinking has been a social custom widely practiced in Ireland for centuries. Moderate consumption of alcohol is often tolerated even during working hours, provided it does not lead to obvious inebriation or obstreperous behaviour. Intoxication that does not significantly affect the performance of duty tends to be overlooked in Ireland, with charitable references to persons being 'two sheets to the wind' or 'a little under the weather'. Seldom does one dare to allege drunkenness, unless the victim is considered with much disdain or belongs to what is perceived to be a lower social order.

In all probability, drunkenness was endemic among railway staff at least during the nineteenth and the first half of the twentieth centuries. The operation of steam trains in that period gave rise to very hard manual work for relatively very low wages. The work was continuous and exhausting, with frequent unsocial hours, night work and long absences from home. It was no surprise, therefore, that relief from boredom and the daily grind was sought in drink. All grades of railway staff seemed to indulge to some extent and 'being under the influence of drink' was the most frequently quoted cause of disciplinary action on the railways in Ireland well into the twentieth century.

Research undertaken by Keith Haines into the causes of the 1871 Ballymacarrett accident in East Belfast has revealed that there were two distilleries in the district at that time stated to be 'for the manufacture of the spirit *craythur*, now so much in demand by the working class people'. There was a proliferation of outlets selling alcohol that prevailed into the twentieth century, particularly in the form of spirit groceries that enthralled many women. Reverend John Redmond, minister of St Patrick's in Ballymacarrett, recorded 82 spirit groceries and 44 public houses in the Mountpottinger sub-district of East Belfast during the early 1920s. Some amusing tales were recorded in Belfast arising from the abuse of alcoholic drink. A couple of weeks after the Ballymacarrett accident, the *Belfast Newsletter* reported that a

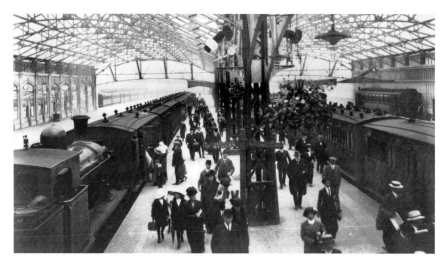

The interior of Queen's Quay terminus of the B&CDR, Belfast in the 1890s. The Bangor train is on the left and the train for Castlewellan on the right. A rail motor train to Hollywood is on the extreme right.

Leslie Bell was:

> charged with having been drunk in charge of a horse and cart in Corporation Street... The prisoner, who attributed all his misfortunes to an excessive kindness of disposition which prevented him from saying no when pressed to drink, was fined ten shillings and costs.

Within days of Thomas Trainor being imprisoned on account of the Ballymacarrett accident, the *Belfast Newsletter* of 31 July 1871 reported that a Mary O'Rorke was charged in the Police Court with cursing the Pope at midnight. Head Constable Lamb expressed the opinion that, if she were discharged, she had nowhere to go and would end up back at the Police Office. The magistrate suggested that, if she liked to live in gaol, she could be sentenced for three months. The grateful Mary O'Rorke was recorded as having responded, 'Thank you your worship. I could stand on my head for that time.'

Following the accident at Ballymacarrett, the local Belfast press began to question the widespread custom of excessive alcohol consumption that led to many unsavoury reports in its columns. Reporting on yet another incident of excessive drinking, the *Belfast Newsletter* of 23 May 1871 lamented that 'the frequency of cases of this character is becoming remarkable, a circumstance which cannot fail to be regarded with regret'. A Belfast surgeon, Norman Barnett, believed that particularly among the lower classes, drunkenness could quickly develop from a habit into a disease and bemoaned the fact that the conservative legal procedure still regarded drunkenness as simply a crime.

He pointed out that the penalty, more often than not, was a fine and then made the following most revealing observation:

> The payment of the fine inflicted in so many cases is often made by the publican, whose customer the prisoner is and much too good a one to lose by his going to prison even for a short period.

According to Keith Haines, the drink culture was by no means confined to railway servants of the lower classes. Intoxication proved to be a problem also for the professional and officer classes of the Belfast & County Down Railway (B&CDR). One of the company's accountants Charles Vosser is recorded as having turned up for work on a number of occasions in 1872 'more or less under the influence of drink'. He was given three months' notice, but appears to have taken umbrage and resigned. Some years later another B&CDR accountant, James Cumming, was asked to account for his unexplained absence from the office and was cautioned as to his future conduct. It is recorded that he undertook 'to leave off living in hotels and provide proper and respectable lodging accommodation for himself'. The accountant failed to live up to his promise and was eventually dismissed when he turned up for work 'in a state unfit for business'.

There was also evidence of a drink culture among officers of the B&CDR. On 23 May 1871, ten days after the Ballymacarrett accident, a Board meeting of the company confirmed the dismissal of the station master at Crossgar who had been intoxicated. Despite his promise of future better conduct, the Board insisted on dismissing him 'as no excuse for this offence will be taken'. In May 1872 the General Manager of the company sacked the station master and four porters at Groomesport for drunkenness and announced that in future 'porters dismissed for such an offence would be presented to the magistrates'. In January 1874 the station master at Tullymurray was discovered drunk in his office and was prosecuted at Seaford Petty Sessions. He was given a two pound fine or a month's hard labour. Even one of the permanent way inspectors was dismissed in October 1874 for being under the influence of drink on duty.

It is difficult to ascertain how strictly B&CDR regulations were applied before the May 1871 accident at Ballymacarrett, but it certainly seemed to result in a more deliberate approach from the company thereafter. But their initial approach to the drink culture was somewhat ambivalent, judging from the request that emanated from the Board meeting held on the Monday following the fatal accident. The Directors requested the General Manager and the Chief Engineer to prepare a report on 'the best means of preventing the possibility of drivers, firemen and guards leaving the stations in a state of intoxication'. No reference was made to any possibility of intoxication among higher grades. A week later, rather lame action was decided on when senior management in response to the Board's request decided 'to have them sign a book on coming on duty and on going off duty'!

The real problem, of course, was that drink was endemic in the culture. Lyn Gallagher, who researched bank personnel in the Ulster Bank, found that:

> There was also an active vigilance about alcohol abuse and inspectors were asked to be particularly vigilant in reporting any evidence of over-indulgence. There is no doubt that there were problems of this sort within the Ulster Bank, especially when an official was moved to a small town away from family, friends and other occupations. Several letters to staff exist which refer to difficulties of this type.

Research conducted by B. Griffin into police in nineteenth-century Belfast found that up to half the cases of disciplinary action taken against constables was as a result of inebriation.

> The impression one gets from the punishments recorded in the police minutes is that drunkenness was very much an occupational hazard for members of the Belfast force. Apart from the early years of the force, the police authorities seem to have accepted the inevitability of police drunkenness and that it would be impossible to dismiss men for just a single instance of inebriety on duty; to do this would have meant having no experienced policemen in the force. In Belfast the municipal authorities may not have been happy with their force's fondness for drink, and signalled their disapproval by dismissing repeated offenders, but they only fined or punished in other ways for most initial infringements.

The exterior of the B&CDR terminus at Queen's Quay, Belfast in the 1890s.

The considerable amount of evidence generated by the 1871 Ballymacarrett accident would strongly suggest that railway companies also displayed a similar benign connivance with the drink culture. Yet the Chairman of the B&CDR was able, on the evening of the accident on 13 May, to order the arrest of the goods train fireman Thomas Trainor and the issuing of a statement indicating that the cause of the accident was directly attributable to the misconduct of just one low-paid railway servant who, when arrested, was found to be in a state of intoxication. One must wonder why that was done?

train at 5.30 a.m. and travelled north to Armagh by way of Portadown. On reaching the latter station the driver was told that, as ticket sales for the excursion were going well, the Armagh station master had requested that the train be strengthened. A further two carriages were added at Portadown, resulting in a train of fifteen vehicles arriving in Armagh about 8.30 a.m.

Tensions Develop

On arrival there the station master John Foster took control. Since the previous day he had realised that the number of passengers for the excursion would significantly exceed 800. He had prepared the necessary extra tickets, but for some reason had not informed headquarters at Dundalk of the increased complement. Had he done so, a stronger six-coupled engine than the four-coupled No 86 could have been provided. When Driver McGrath arrived with his train of fifteen carriages, station master Foster proposed that perhaps two or three more should be added. The driver adamantly refused, pointing out that his instructions from Dundalk were to take only thirteen carriages. According to evidence given during later investigations, the station master curtly replied, 'I did not write those instructions for you.' The driver responded, 'Mr Cowan wrote them,' adding a query, 'Why did you not send proper word to Dundalk and I would have a proper six-coupled engine with me?' Stung by this accusation of neglect of his duties, Station Master Foster retorted, 'Any driver that comes here does not grumble about taking an excursion train with him.' These exchanges sparked tension between the worried driver and the authoritarian station master that most probably contributed to the subsequent tragedy.

Passengers who heard the exchanges gave evidence that Driver McGrath turned on his heel and walked away down the platform, clearly indignant that his professional expertise as a driver had been doubted by the Armagh station master. He seemed particularly annoyed that this doubt had been cast in the presence of another key participant James Elliott, Chief Assistant to the Traffic Manager, who had come from Dundalk to take overall control of the excursion. Chief Assistant Elliott, who had long experience of conducting excursion trains, tried to offer a helpful suggestion. No 9, the engine of the ordinary morning train to Newry scheduled to follow the excursion some thirty minutes later, could be used to give extra power by helping to push the excursion train from the rear up to the top of the first long steep gradient about three miles southeast of Armagh. When Chief Assistant Elliott and Station Master Foster put this suggestion to Driver McGrath, he dismissed it saying, 'I have great confidence in the engine I have.' Behind the driver's indignant refusal of any assistance from another engine lay the slur cast earlier by the station master on his own professional competence.

Children arriving at a station for an excursion to the seaside in Co Down.

The Excursion Sets Off

Meanwhile the passengers began to arrive for their exciting trip to the seaside. Members of the Sunday School party marched in procession from the Methodist Church in Abbey Street to the railway station, headed by the band of the Third Battalion of the Royal Irish Fusiliers, then stationed at Gough Barracks in Armagh. Other participants made their own various ways to the station. In festive mood the passengers were loaded into the carriage compartments and, as their tickets were checked, the doors of their compartments were locked at the request of the organisers to prevent people without tickets getting aboard. In subsequent investigations, however, it became apparent that the doors of the train, or most of them, were locked on both sides. Nobody afterwards would admit having given such orders or hearing anyone else give them. It was fairly certain that the empty train, when it arrived from Dundalk, had its doors locked and that the platform side had been re-locked as the compartments became full. The consequences of this action were to prove fatal to many.

At 10.15, a quarter of an hour late, the excursion was at last ready to leave. A total of 941 tickets had been issued and Station Master Foster estimated that children made up about two-thirds of the total. The other third were teachers, stewards and guardians. Of the 600 children aboard, about 150 were estimated to have been less than five-years old. As soon as the signal was given Driver McGrath put on full steam, the engine's driving wheels began to turn, slipped momentarily, regained their grip and the train moved forward. Cheers of delight arose from the tightly-packed carriages as the happy trippers set off for their day by the sea. For some distance the train travelled well, but at the first steep portion of the incline it began to reduce speed. As it came to the steeper 1 in 75 gradient, its progress became slower and slower until finally it stopped near Dobbin's Bridge, about 200m short of the summit. Its speed on the journey from Armagh had averaged 11 mph. The time was now 10.33, just two minutes before the scheduled departure time from Armagh of the ordinary train to Newry, headed by No 9. That train was totally unaware that the preceding train had stalled before reaching the summit of the first hill just three miles away.

The Train's Brake System
To understand the basic cause of the ensuing calamity, it is necessary to appreciate the brake system of trains at that time. During the nineteenth century the Board of Trade supervised railway operation in both Britain and Ireland. Several serious accidents in Britain had moved interested parties to speak out on the problem of stopping trains in an emergency and, under Board of Trade auspices, the important Newark Trials were held in 1875 to test different types of brakes. Two years later the Board of Trade sent a circular to all railway companies stating a set of conditions which a satisfactory brake should meet and urging for safety reasons that all passengers trains be fitted with continuous brakes, either the automatic or non-automatic system, as soon as possible.

There was an important difference between the two systems. An automatic system ensured that, should a train be divided, the continuous brake would instantly be applied to all carriages. The non-automatic did not have this desirable quality, but it was not as expensive a system to have fitted to all engines and passenger vehicles.

The GNR had adopted Smith's non-automatic brake system in 1878, in which brake blocks operated on each of the driving and trailing wheels of the engine and on each of the coal tender's wheels. The carriages had two brake blocks on each wheel of the outer axles and under the frames of vehicles were leather bags which, when deflated, applied the brakes. Additional braking power for the train was provided by the handbrake in the guard's van. The Smith system was adopted by many railway companies because it did not require constant steam to operate it. Steam was only required to apply the brakes, whereas the automatic system used steam to keep the brakes off. But there was a serious drawback with the simpler brake system. When the flexible brake-pipes between carriages were parted, the brakes in the detached carriages would not work on the application of steam. The GNR and other companies, however, were prepared to overlook this defect because the Smith Vacuum Brake was cheaper and simpler to operate.

The Disaster Unfolds

When the excursion train stalled just before reaching the summit at Dobbin's Bridge, Fireman Parkinson shovelled more coal on to the fire and went around the engine with an oil-can to look for a cause of the stall. Driver McGrath decided it was quite unrealistic to expect No 86 to restart with such a heavy load. Chief Assistant Elliott, who had overall control of the excursion, agreed with the driver's view and suggested dividing the train so that the front portion could be brought forward about two miles to the first station at Hamilton's Bawn, where five carriages could be left in a siding. The chief assistant then decided to divide the train between the fifth and sixth vehicles. First he went back along the track to the other end of the train and asked the back guard Thomas Henry if the brakes were on. When assured that this task had already been attended to, he asked the guard to leave his van and set stones under its wheels. Chief Assistant Elliott then returned to watch the uncoupling of the carriages by the front guard William Moorhead, after he had placed a stone against one of the wheels of the sixth vehicle so that it would remain steady when detached from the front portion of the train.

The essential point to note is that, when the coupling connection and air pipe had been parted, the non-automatic vacuum brake was released. Therefore, the ten carriages now detached from the front portion of the train were in the perilous position of having only the handbrake in the guard's van and the stones placed under the wheels to hold them on the steep incline. These might well have been enough as long as the vehicles received no disturbance or sudden shock.

Chief Assistant Elliott then sent Front Guard Moorhead forward to instruct the driver to start for Hamilton's Bawn with the front portion of the train, but to take care not to allow the engine to move backwards before starting. The front guard obeyed this order and testified later that when he released his handbrake he felt the van move backwards. Attached to it of course were four carriages that struck against the sixth carriage with a force sufficient to dislodge the single stone placed at its wheel. The motion ran back through the other carriages, all of which, other than the rear brake van, were now free of any brake application. The accumulating shock wave on reaching the rear van was enough to crush the stones and overcome its brake blocks, whether or not they were even still effective in trying to hold the weight of ten full carriages on a steep incline.

The entire rear portion now began to move off down the hill. The Front

Guard Moorhead tried in vain to run after the carriages when they first started to move, in the hope of re-coupling the train, but he tripped over some old rails lying beside the track. The increasing speed of the detached carriages soon made it impossible to do anything more. Within these carriages, behind locked doors, were hundreds of trapped passengers.

Towards the Horrific Collision

Meanwhile the ordinary morning train to Newry, headed by engine No 9 whose assistance Driver McGrath had earlier refused, was preparing to depart from Armagh at 10.35 but was delayed by the late arrival of a connection from Belfast. At this point it should be explained that, as traffic over the line to Newry was light, the GNR saw no reason for unnecessary expense on a high standard signalling system. Instead of the Block System, which allowed only one train at a time to enter a section between stations on single-track lines, the company used the Train Staff and Ticket System. This cheaper system allowed a staff to be carried by the engine driver as his authority to enter a single-track section. If a second train was to follow in the same direction, a ticket was handed to the first driver and the staff shown to him to let him see it was properly available for the section and the staff was given to the driver of the second train to carry with him. The first staff section from Armagh was to Markethill, a distance of some nine miles. As a further safeguard on the Armagh to Newry line, the GNR used the Time Interval System whereby a following train had to wait a specified time before moving

Engine No 9 on a typical Armagh-Newry line train in the 1890s.

The Armagh disaster.

off. The intervals on this line were passenger train after passenger ten minutes and passenger after goods train twenty minutes.

By the time the ordinary train was ready to leave Armagh it was 10.39, well beyond the regulation interval. No 9 and its short train of a horsebox, four carriages and a brake van left Armagh and was soon breasting the gradient. Going well, the train reached the high embankment at Killuney about two miles out when the fireman William Herd shouted to his driver Patrick Murphy that something was coming down the line. Rushing to the right-hand side of the cab, both men saw to their horror the terrifying sight of a rake of carriages coming out of a cutting and bearing down on them along the embankment at high speed. The fireman immediately put No 9 into reverse gear and gave the engine backsteam, while the driver put on the vacuum brake so hard that he managed to reduce speed to less than 5 mph.

The runaway carriages, estimated to be travelling at 40 mph by this stage, crashed into No 9 with such appalling force that the engine was thrown off the rails and landed down at the side of the track. The destruction was terrible. Three vehicles were totally demolished, their wreckage strewn over both sides of the embankment and their wheels and axles scattered. The rest of the carriages managed to stay upright, but some were derailed and many passengers in these were hurt. But in the wreckage of the destroyed carriages 73 people were killed outright and many others were very badly injured, suffering severe shock and mutilations of the severest kind.

Just before the crash Fireman Herd jumped clear of No 9, escaping with a fall down the embankment and only slight injuries. Driver Murphy had turned around and grasped the coal tender. The collision divided the engine from the tender and broke the coupling behind the horsebox. However, the coal tender and other vehicles remained on the rails and began to run back downhill. The guard of the train Daniel Graham, although thrown down and dazed from the collision, recovered himself and used his handbrake to stop the carriages before they could reach Armagh station. Following down the hill was the horsebox and the coal tender but, with Driver Murphy still clinging on to the tender, he managed to apply the tender handbrake and bring the two vehicles to rest just a few yards short of the remainder of No 9's train. The bravery of these men prevented an even worse disaster in Armagh that day.

The Aftermath

The point of collision with the runaway carriages was about two miles from Armagh at Killuney on a steeply-graded embankment over 45 feet above ground. The ten carriages had travelled over two miles downhill before they collided violently with the following train. The station master at Armagh was the first to suspect that something had gone wrong, when he received a telegraphic message about 11.00 a.m. from Markethill that the excursion train had not yet arrived there. Very soon afterwards he saw the distraught Chief Assistant Elliott come running down the line from the scene of the collision to tell the horrific news. The alarm was quickly spread and all the help the city and county could give was summoned. Everyone who could supply aid or transport did so. Telegrams were dispatched by Station Master Foster to the neighbouring towns of Portadown, Lurgan, Tynan and Glaslough and even as far away as the city of Belfast to summon more doctors. The doctors and resources of Armagh Infirmary were overstretched and had to be augmented by much private benevolence. People everywhere were moved to pity and charity and money was generously given to assist those who had been injured or bereaved.

Messages had also been sent to Gough Barracks and to the Royal Irish Constabulary, who formed strong parties to set off on foot to the scene of the disaster with full ambulance equipment. Among them was a contingent from the Royal Irish Fusiliers whose Third Battalion band was on the train. When they arrived at the scene, they first had to extricate people from the wreckage and separate the living from the dead. Those beyond human aid were laid out in the fields below the embankment and every available conveyance in Armagh was requisitioned for the removal of the dead and the seriously injured to the city. A large number had sustained their injuries in falling from the train as they attempted to save themselves. Some of those not badly hurt made their way home on foot, dazed and horrified. The Sunday School teachers and guardians who were unhurt assisted in the rescue, but had to exercise extreme care in removing casualties from derailed carriages perilously balanced on the edge of the high embankment.

To appreciate the enormous traumatic impact the disaster had on contemporary society, it is worth quoting an extract from the editorial of the *Belfast Newsletter* on 12 June 1889 that described the accident as:

> the most appalling catastrophe of the kind which has ever taken place in the North of Ireland. It has plunged a city into profound mourning, for the appearance of some quarters of Armagh last night suggested that visitation of remote antiquity of which it is recorded that 'there was not a house in which there was not one dead'. In the neighbourhood of those public buildings which have been used as temporary morgues and surgeries, the scene last night resembled such as one can imagine occurring when some form of deadly pestilence has been raging unchecked and has converted a prosperous city into a charnel-house. As the ghastly burdens were borne along the road during the afternoon and evening the gloom overhanging the city became greater.

The memorial in Armagh Methodist church for Sunday School teacher, Samuel Steel, who died in the 1889 rail disaster.

Inside the newspapers were full of accounts of the accident, insofar as details were then clear. There were eulogies of a prominent victim, the deceased Petty Sessions Clerk Samuel Steel, and a report that five out of the ten members of the Cleeland family were dead, including both father and mother. Another death not directly concerned with the accident was reported, that of John Hughes an aged cab driver of Armagh who took out a party of rescuers and was so overcome by the sight that he collapsed and died. It was presumed he had some relatives on the crashed train.

Another most moving contemporary account of the aftermath of the accident was given by Surgeon-Major J. M. Lynn in a letter published in the *Belfast Newsletter* on Monday, 17 June 1889. He travelled on the train with the children and the following extract from his letter paints a horrific picture:

> When the collision occurred I was confounded and could not grasp the awful nature of our position, but when I saw the engine off the rails and volumes of steam issuing out of the burst boiler and heard the groans and

crying of the dying, I was so paralysed I could hardly get out of the carriage. I then for some time attended to the wounded, but at last I was so overcome with the awful sights with which I was surrounded, that I was exhausted. Providentially the Armagh doctors now came to our relief. The frightful appearance of many of the dear children who were crushed to death by the rush of the locomotive into their cars, or burned to death by the fire from the engine or scalded to death by hot steam, was most appalling. Some of them were quite unrecognisable, save by the clothes which they wore, and even these were in many cases torn into fragments. Many by leaping out of the carriages and falling down the high embankment on which the collision occurred, were severely wounded and some killed.

In no part of the kingdom has ever such an overwhelming calamity occurred. Many a bitterly-fought battlefield did not display such a carnage. The entire matter is to me a most mysterious Providence.

The fact that the boiler had not burst did not render this letter any less poignant. Surgeon-Major Lynn had returned to his native city to retire after a military career and was a man highly respected in Armagh.

The Official Reaction

News of the collision had reached Dundalk by 11.40 and half-an-hour later a breakdown train left for the scene of the crash by way of Portadown and Armagh. Included in the party that travelled on the train were the Deputy Chairman of the GNR James Gray, a Director Foster Coates, the Northern Section Manager Thomas Shaw, the Southern Section Manager J. D. Cowan, and the Locomotive Engineer James Crawford Park. They reached the scene at 2.10 p.m. and immediately began the work of clearing the line except for No 9, which was left where it lay pending the arrival of the Inspecting Officer from the Board of Trade. Another gang of men arrived from Belfast to assist in the clearance. Before that work began, District Inspector Bonis of the Portadown Royal Irish Constabulary had the wreckage thoroughly photographed for use in the subsequent inquiries. Some of these photographs have survived to illustrate the present text.

In the afternoon, James Elliot, Thomas McGrath, Henry Parkinson and William Moorhead were arrested at the scene of the disaster by District Inspector Bonis and lodged in custody.

The Coroner's Inquest

As news of the extent of the calamity spread, indignation and alarm seized the public. It was widely believed that someone had blundered and the hunt began almost at once to identify and lay blame on the culprits. An inquest on the victims was opened by the Crown Coroner for Armagh T. G. Peel the evening of the very day of the accident, when the jury was charged with 'investigating when, where and by what means the deceased had come to their deaths'. The scene of the disaster was visited by the jury and the bodies viewed but, apart from hearing formal evidence of identification, little further progress could be made until after the arrival of the expected investigating officer from the Board of Trade. The inquest had to be adjourned that evening, but continued to meet in the following days with several more adjournments.

Like many coroner's inquests, it strayed out of its proper field and much of the evidence given covered a wide area of railway operation and practice. Public anger was evident in the jurors' questioning of witnesses, especially the GNR and some of its staff. GNR rules concerning the locking of carriage doors and the earlier proposal to raise the excursion fare were questioned. It will be recalled that the GNR later relented on the fare rise, on the condition that ticket sales would be restricted to members of the Methodist Church. It was interesting how it emerged that this condition had been flouted. The religious affiliations of the first 76 victims identified after the collision revealed that 34 were members of the Church of Ireland, 19 were Presbyterians, 5 were Roman Catholics and only 18 were members of the Methodist Church.

There was considerable anger also over the fact that James Elliott and other persons then in custody could not attend the inquest to give evidence. An established practice since the Marquess of Hartington's period as Chief

Armagh Gaol, built in 1780, where James Elliott was imprisoned.

Secretary for Ireland required that persons charged with manslaughter should not attend inquests. Under pressure, however, an application was made on 15 June to the Lord Chief Justice of Ireland in the Queen's Bench Division in Dublin for a writ of *habeas corpus* for James Elliott, then languishing in Armagh Gaol. The Crown Counsel on this occasion was the famous Edward Carson, who later moved to Belfast to lead the Ulster Unionists in their resistance to Home Rule. The writ was granted and James Elliott subsequently attended the inquest, gave evidence and was examined.

On 20 June a letter from the Secretary of the GNR was read to the inquest in which the directors expressed their profound regret at the disastrous accident on 12 June, conveyed their heartfelt sympathy to the sufferers, their relatives and their friends, and assured them that it was the unanimous decision of the Board that all circumstances connected with the terrible disaster should receive the fullest investigation. The letter ended with a statement that the directors would not raise any question as to the liability of the company and were prepared to consider fully any claims that may be made on behalf of those who may have suffered by the accident. By that statement, the GNR had virtually conceded liability for the accident.

The very next day, Friday 21 June, just nine days after the disaster, the jury returned with a remarkable verdict:

James C. Park, guilty of culpable negligence in not having proper supervision in the selection of the engine. William Fenton, culpable negligence in the selection of the engine. James Elliott, culpable negligence in having ordered part of the train to be uncoupled without having ascertained that the rear part of the train was secure. Thomas Henry, negligence in not having applied the brake properly. Thomas McGrath, negligence in the discharge of his duty. William Moorhead, negligence in the discharge of his duty.

The coroner then clarified that the verdict was manslaughter against Messrs Park, Elliott, Henry, McGrath and Moorhead. William Fenton was excluded, as James Park was his superior. Bail was accepted for the latter but the others remained in custody, except for Thomas Henry who was still in Armagh Infirmary.

The jury raised significant issues in their long list of recommendations. The principal one was that the government would soon enforce by legislation the use by all railway companies of the automatic continuous vacuum brake, as its use would have prevented the Armagh collision. They also recommended that special precautions be taken in running excursion trains and that the management of the GNR headquarters at Dundalk should be reorganised to establish clear lines of authority. However, little official attention was given to the local views strongly expressed in the inquest verdict and recommendations. The Crown was more concerned with sending James Elliott, Thomas McGrath, Henry Parkinson and William Moorhead for trial.

Outrage in Dundalk

The people of Dundalk were outraged at the treatment of Chief Assistant to the Traffic Manager James Elliott. He was a man of reputation in Dundalk, as much respected as was the Petty Sessions Clerk Samuel Steele in Armagh. The *Dundalk Democrat* believed that too much responsibility had been thrown on James Elliott's shoulders, that he was overworked and was a classic case of the willing horse. It continued:

> His zeal in the company's service made him always ready for work. A most exemplary young man, ever sober and grave in manner beyond his years, he was still possessed of the most genial temperament. Most business people in Dundalk must be aware that for many years in all matters connected with the traffic Mr Elliott was the person to make satisfactory arrangements and his desire to facilitate problems between the company and its customers was patent to everyone. The horrible calamity which has left so many people desolated is accentuated by the fact that a young man so full of good report as Mr Elliott should appear, from common rumour, to be the innocent cause.

Within a short time a number of friends set up a fund for the defence of James Elliott and, following publication of a letter from four prominent businessmen in the *Dundalk Democrat* of 29 June, a public fund was instituted for the defence of their townsmen and to secure a fair trial.

By early August the fund had reached £150, of which a third had come from railway men in England. This sum was apportioned, £45 each to the three Dundalk men James Elliott, Thomas McGrath and Thomas Henry, and £15 to William Moorhead, a Newry man. The latter item enraged another Dundalk newspaper, *The Herald*, which asked why should not the people of Newry look after their own. A letter published in the same newspaper from a Dundalk citizen raised a further interesting point. What must the people of Armagh think when they saw Dundalk people raising money for the defence of those whom they must regard as the guilty parties, instead of contributing to the Armagh Relief Fund?

The Criminal Trial

Just before the inquest opened on 12 June, the four arrested at the scene of the disaster and lodged in custody were brought before the Armagh Resident Magistrate and charged provisionally with 'having with negligence and

originally-intended thirteen vehicles, and had also sent a driver who was inexperienced and had never previously driven over the difficult Armagh to Newry line. He attached no blame to the fireman Henry Parkinson or to either of the guards Thomas Henry and William Moorhead who had acted under James Elliott's orders. Major General Hutchinson had words of great commendation for the crew of the following ordinary passenger train and for their action after the collision in preventing another runaway from happening.

Having indicated the degree of culpability he believed attached to the railway officials involved in the disaster, the Investigating Officer turned to the means that could be adopted to guard against the recurrence of any similar calamity in future:

> This terrible collision would in all human probability have been prevented had the excursion train been fitted with an automatic continuous vacuum brake, instead of, as it was, with only a non-automatic vacuum brake... As the President of the Board of Trade has stated in Parliament his intention to introduce a Bill to make compulsory the adoption of automatic continuous brakes, should the report on this collision point out that it would have been avoided had the excursion train been fitted with them, it is unnecessary for me to say any more upon the subject.

With regard to the signalling system on the Armagh to Newry line, Major General Hutchinson also reached a significant conclusion:

> It seems manifest that if the block telegraph system had been in force between Armagh and Hamilton's Bawn, the results of this collision would have been considerably mitigated, and it becomes subsequently a grave question whether legislative power should not be sought to make the block system compulsory on old lines, as it has been for many years past on new ones.

The report concluded with a condemnation of the running of such heavy excursion trains over such a difficult line and recommended that in future they should be limited to ten vehicles.

The Report's Impact on the GNR

Publication of the Board of Trade's report on 7 November 1889 brought about major changes in the GNR. The Board of Directors decided immediately to appoint a general manager for the first time and to ask for the resignation of J. D. Cowan, Southern Traffic Manager in Dundalk, who had been in effect the superintendent of the line. After much prolonged negotiations, the post of the first General Manager of the GNR was given to Thomas Robertson from the Highland Railway in Scotland in April 1890.

This ebullient personality soon made his mark felt on the GNR and on Irish railways generally. By the time he left to become the Chairman of the Irish Board of Works in 1896, the GNR had been transformed. It had begun to fit the automatic vacuum brake to all its passenger locomotives and rolling stock in September 1890 and this considerable task was completed within two years. Strict block working and interlocking signalling was also enforced within three years on the entire GNR mainline and on all branches, including the Armagh to Newry line.

The Legacy of the Armagh Disaster

Within a few days of the Armagh collision, the President of the Board of Trade announced that the government would at once introduce a Bill in parliament at Westminster for the purpose of bringing the law of railway safety up to date. He hoped that parliament would pass the measure into law without delay, as a non-controversial matter. The minister was quite confident that his hope would be realised as legislation of this kind had been called for over the previous decade, but to no avail.

The political theory in Victorian Britain was one of *laissez faire* or non-interference of government in private business. Since 1878, however, concerned voices had been raised at Westminster about railway safety and the need for government to impose stricter safety standards on private railway companies. In particular, Mr F. A. Channing the radical MP for Northamptonshire East had been assiduous in raising questions about railway happenings that he believed deserved attention. He had focused especially on two previous accidents that had occurred on the GNR involving runaway vehicles. These incidents resembled the accident at Armagh, but fortunately did not result in any loss of life. A mixed train conveying both passengers and goods became divided when travelling between Beragh and Omagh in Co Tyrone in 1878 and in the same year a coupling of the coal tender on a passenger express to Belfast broke between Skerries and Balbriggan in Co Dublin, causing the detached carriages to roll down a slight incline towards the engine and tender as they were returning to reconnect with their train.

When the Board of Trade wrote to the GNR after these serious incidents occurred in 1878, the company replied that the continuous vacuum brake was still regarded as being experimental and that no decision had yet been reached about it. Yet, eleven years later, the GNR was still using the non-automatic brake with tragic consequences. Indeed, only three weeks after the terrible Armagh disaster, another runaway happened near Goraghwood in Co Armagh when a goods train became divided on a steep incline and some twenty wagons rolled back downhill a distance of almost ten miles before coming to a stop near Poyntzpass. These unsettling events greatly increased pressure at Westminster and finally on 15 July 1889 the President of the Board of Trade, Sir Michael Hicks-Beach Bt, introduced a Bill to amend the then existing law to require railway companies to use certain coupling apparatus. That Bill became law as the Regulation of Railways Act 1889 on 30 August.

Section One of the 1889 Act was of the utmost importance. It gave the Board of Trade power to order railway companies to do, within a time limited by the order, any of the following things:

(a) To adopt the block system on all or any of their railways open for the conveyance of passengers;

(b) To provide for the interlocking of points and signals on or in connection with all or any of such railways;

(c) To provide for and use on all their trains carrying passengers continuous brakes complying with the following requirements, namely:

    (i) The brake must be instantaneous in action and capable of being applied by the engine driver and guards;

    (ii) The brake must be self-applying in the event of any failure in the continuity of its action;

    (iii) The brake must be capable of being applied to every vehicle of the train, whether carrying passengers or not;

    (iv) The brake must be in regular use in daily working;

    (v) The materials of the brake must be of a durable character and easily maintained and kept in order.

While changes have been made since the Regulation of Railways Act 1889, all have been minor ones to suit changing times. But the basic framework of the Act still applies to this day.

This legislation arising directly out of the Armagh collision marked a watershed in railway history. It heralded the end of the *laissez faire* railway policy of non-intervention of government in private companies and brought their operating methods under closer official scrutiny. From the Act of 1889 stemmed better regulations and inventions, the spirit of which is still evident on Irish railways. In recent years we have seen a wonderful flowering of science in rail safety equipment and now take for granted the efficiency of signalling and its inbuilt precautions against mishaps. When travelling on Ireland's modern and fast railway services today we should never forget the legacy of the Armagh Disaster of 1889, which has ensured that all modern railway vehicles are now fitted with continuous automatic vacuum brakes.

DERRY TRAGEDY

On the Londonderry & Lough Swilly Railway a head-on collision occurred on 21 June 1891 at Springtown just one mile outside Derry/*Doire* between a special troop train travelling to Letterkenny and an in-coming empty train. The latter train subsequently was found to have improperly started from Tooban Junction for Derry, for reasons that scarcely seem credible today.

The customary inquiry into the collision described the troop train as being hauled by 2-4-0T engine No 5 running bunker-first, followed by 'two wagons loaded with baggage, a wagon conveying a horse, seven carriages, a brake van and two wagons of light luggage, thirteen vehicles in all, in the order given'. The brake power consisted of a handbrake for the four-coupled wheels of the engine and another handbrake for the brake van, in which there was a guard. There were between 250 and 300 militiamen on board, fourteen of whom were injured. The engine crew escaped injury by jumping for their lives. The empty train, consisting of a brake van and two carriages headed by 0-6-2T engine No 2, was also running bunker-first but it collided with such force with the heavy troop train that its two engine crew were killed outright.

Incredibly, the subsequent inquiry revealed that the signalman at Tooban Junction who had authorised the departure of the empty train for Derry could neither read nor write. He was therefore understandably vague about the running of the troop special. When questioned at the Assize Court, he explained how he dealt with written instructions:

> When a written message is sent me, I get different persons to read it, sometimes passengers and sometimes men belonging to the road.

Asked who read the message given to him on the day of that fatal accident, he said:

> Dan Doherty, a neighbour; he could not make out something at the bottom and then I got Mary Ann Quigley to read it. There was some part she could not make out. I went to no one after that.

Derry train at Tooban Junction. The 1891 tragedy was caused by action taken in the signal box at the platform end.

In consequence of this rather haphazard operating method, two men tragically lost their lives in the collision. Subsequently, the Tooban Junction signalman was dismissed by the Londonderry & Lough Swilly Railway Company.

THE CAMP DISASTER

Dingle/*An Daingean*, Co Kerry is said to be the town in Europe nearest to America, being situated almost at the southwestern tip of Ireland. Because of its location at the extremity of a very mountainous peninsula, Dingle was served for some sixty years by a railway cheaply-built to a gauge of three feet rather than a normal heavy-rail line built to the standard Irish gauge of five feet three inches. Following three years of construction the thirty-one mile Tralee & Dingle Railway was opened in 1891, with a five-mile branch to Castlegregory, but it did not meet with universal approval. The *Ward Guide to Ireland* published shortly after the opening gave its readers the following advice:

> The cautious traveller will go by rail to Castlegregory and thence by road over Connor Hill to Dingle. He will thus avoid a none-too-safe bit of railway. It is much to be regretted that the Dingle line was not made of full gauge and on safe inclines.

The wisdom of this advice was vindicated in the tragic story of the special train returning from the Dingle Pig Fair on 22 May 1893.

On the day of the Pig Fair in 1893 the railway was very busy. All of the company's steam locomotives, carriages and wagons were pressed into service to cater for the traffic. The staff were so hard pressed that the company's recently appointed Locomotive Inspector, Alfred Redshaw of Lancashire, was instructed to drive the heavily-laden special train to Tralee, even though he had little knowledge or experience of the difficulties of controlling a train over the steep inclines and treacherous curves of the line. The train left Dingle at 1.30 p.m., over half-an-hour late, with seven laden wagons of pigs, one passenger coach and a brake van. The coach was carrying 38 pig buyers and representatives from Denny's and Lunham's bacon factories.

At the first stop, Lispole, Driver Redshaw was heard having a loud

A double-headed cattle train near Camp climbing a 1 in 35 gradient on the Tralee-Dingle railway.

argument with Guard Thomas O'Leary as to whether the vacuum brake should be on or off. At the next stop, Annascaul, the train overshot the platform and had to reverse. But beyond Annascaul began the steep six-mile ascent of 1 in 29 up the western mountain slope and it was here that the trouble really began. Whether because the load was too heavy or the engine was in poor condition, the ascent took nearly two hours, with several stops. One survivor of that tragic journey stated: 'We had a bad hill, a bad line, a bad engine and a bad driver.'

About 4.30 p.m. the train reached the summit at Glenagalt/*Gleann na nGealt*, the Irish language name ominously meaning 'Valley of the Mad'. Driver Redshaw, who had been looking very fatigued and worried at the last stop, was now thought by those who closely observed him to have lost his head. Guard O'Leary swore at the subsequent inquiry that the vacuum brake was on, but in spite of that the train began to career down the 1 in 31 incline. Hurtling towards Camp/*An Cam* some three miles below, the pig buyers were thrown from side to side in their carriage and in the rear brake van, where nine of them were travelling contrary to company rules. The guard shouted that the train was a runaway and there was immediate panic in the van. One young man named Power jumped out and miraculously survived. From a distant field a man named Darcy saw the train rush down the slope towards the sharply curving bridge at Curraduff. The next moment, he saw only a tangled mass of steel and timber and dying pigs in the Finglas stream below.

The engine hit the parapet of the masonry bridge, crashed through it and toppled into the valley, bringing all the seven pig wagons with it. Driver

The Camp Disaster wreckage below Curraduff Bridge, 1893. Note the dead pigs at the lower left of the picture.

Redshaw was shot into the air and hurled into a mass of debris. Fireman Richard Dillon was found dying underneath the engine and the body of Permanent Way Inspector Bernard O'Loughlin, a native of Limerick, was found some distance away. Upwards of 100 pigs were killed. The passenger coach hung precariously over the edge but did not fall into the valley. Three people were killed, thirteen were seriously injured, and others were bruised and shocked.

Guard O'Leary, who was not badly hurt, realised, with great presence of mind, that the passenger train from Dingle was due in a very short time. Leaving the terrible scenes of horror around him, he immediately rushed back along the line to meet the oncoming train and he succeeded in stopping it. Thomas O'Leary, whose son was later station master at Castlegregory Junction for many years, received great praise for his action. The injured pig buyers were brought down the valley from Curraduff Bridge near Camp to Castlegregory Junction in Lower Camp, from where they were brought back to Tralee by the engine of the Castlegregory branch train.

Scenes of great anguish and anger followed the crash. It was reported that when news of the disaster reached Tralee, a thousand people gathered in the station there. Driver Redshaw's English wife and two children made a heartrending sight. A great sense of public indignation arose against the directors of the Tralee & Dingle Railway Company and it was reported that the police had to be called to prevent deeds of violence. At the official inquiry into the cause of the accident, this indignation was further fuelled by a representative of the company foolishly hinting that the accident might have been caused by residents of Camp putting soap on the line and thereby preventing the train's wheels from gripping. Solicitor Harrington acting for Tralee Town Council was prompted to respond: 'The people of Camp can't buy soap to wash themselves, not to mind putting it on a railway!'

In the course of time public resentment died down, especially as the company began to apply stricter rules for operating the line. Special regulations were introduced requiring all trains in future to take great care on the steep descent to Camp, where every train now had to stop dead before restarting slowly towards the three-chain radius curve over Curraduff Bridge. Yet this solution proved only a temporary remedy. The company soon decided it would be safer to build a lengthy deviation of the line further up the valley with much less severe gradients and curves. On the deviation it provided a new iron viaduct over the Finglas stream. This new Camp Viaduct replaced Curraduff Bridge and was in use until the Tralee & Dingle Railway finally closed in 1953.

A somewhat gruesome footnote may be added. After the tragedy, it emerged that six pigs escaped uninjured at Curraduff. But *The Irish Times* sadly reported on 26 May 1893: 'A consignment of six uninjured pigs, survivors of the dread crash at Camp on Monday, was today received in the Cork Bacon Factory of Messrs Lunham's.'

Pigs being driven to Lunham's bacon factory in Cork, to which the surviving pigs of the Camp Disaster were consigned in 1893.

STORMS IN WEST CLARE

The West Clare Railway, celebrated in Percy French's humourous song 'Are Ye Right There, Michael?', had a greater claim to fame than bad time-keeping, as no less than five trains on that railway were blown off the tracks by high winds and storms. The line was built as a narrow-gauge light railway under the Tramways and Public Companies (Ireland) Act 1883 and was formed by the amalgamation of two separate companies. The West Clare Railway built its line westwards from Ennis to Ennistymon and then southwards to Milltown Malbay, while the South Clare Railway built its lines from Kilkee and Kilrush northwards to Milltown Malbay. This amalgamation resulted in a lengthy stretch of light railway running almost alongside the rugged West Clare coastline exposed to the full severity of Atlantic storms. A most remarkable fact in the history of the West Clare Railway is that nobody was ever killed and few were ever injured in any of the trains blown off the tracks in storms.

Only three years after opening, the West Clare Railway had its first encounter with the wild elements of the Atlantic seaboard. On 14 December 1895, during a severe westerly gale at night, two carriages and a brake van were literally blown out of Kilkee/ *Cill Chaoi* station by the force of the wind. They were discovered the following morning at Moyasta Bridge near Moyasta Junction, a distance of some five miles from Kilkee. They left a trail of destruction behind them, having smashed through no less than six sets of level crossing gates. The storm must have abated by the time the rolling stock reached Moyasta Bridge, which was one of the most exposed places between Kilkee and Kilrush where such light carriages could easily have been blown off the rails in a severe storm.

Early in 1899 a violent storm raged all along the west coast of Ireland causing two trains on the West Clare line to be blown off the rails. At the height of this storm on 12 January, the 9.55 a.m. branch train from Kilrush to Kilkee headed by 0-6-0T engine No 3 'Clifden' was hauling two carriages

An unidentified engine derailed in the 1890s on the West Clare railway.

and two brake vans some two miles from Kilrush when the gale blew the carriages off the rails and on to the side of the line. The engine and vans remained on the tracks. Fortunately, there was only one passenger on board and he escaped injury. Later that same day, the 8.30 a.m. from Ennis headed by 2-6-2T engine No 9 'Fergus' hauling three carriages and a brake van was approaching Quilty/*Coillte* when struck by a violent gust that blew the three carriages and a van completely off the rails and down a ten-metre incline. The engine remained on the line, as the coupling between it and the leading carriage gave way. Fortunately, there were only two passengers on the train by the time it approached Quilty and only one of these received slight injuries.

Subsequent to these incidents, the Board of Trade ordered that in future trains should not be run on exposed sections, such as those around Quilty, during heavy gales unless the stability of the carriages could be improved. For its part, the company lowered the bed of the railway for some 100m on either side of Brews Bridge, erected a windbreaker and raised a protecting embankment by a metre for a distance of some 200m.

Some ten years later, on 17 February 1910, a terrible storm raged in West Clare damaging Kilrush station and tearing up the entire paling at Doonbeg station from its foundations. On that morning the 8.30 a.m. from Ennis headed by 2-6-2T engine No 9 'Fergus' hauling seven wagons, two carriages and a brake van in that order, battled against a strong headwind until it reached Cullinagh Bridge that crossed a public road at an exposed spot near Ennistymon/*Inis Díomáin*. Here the full force of the terrific gale hit the train. Just as the brake van was on the bridge, a sudden squall from the south-west swept the carriages and the wagons off the rails and swung the van against the parapet of the bridge. The coupling between the fourth and fifth wagons broke, but the engine and four wagons remained on the line. The third-class carriage, in which most of the twenty-one passengers on the train were travelling, fell to the bottom of the embankment over six metres deep at this point. The couplings held the second composite carriage suspended by the side of the track. Although the carriages were smashed into matchwood and the wagons badly damaged, it was miraculous that only one passenger received slight injuries. A contributing factor was the fact that Driver Tom Shannon approached Cullinagh Bridge at a very slow speed and this enabled him to bring the train quickly to a halt when the accident happened. Fireman Bernard Maloney later described the aftermath:

> I found Joe Anderson, the guard, turned upside down in the van and he was slightly dazed when I pulled him out. All the passengers in the compo coach got out on the permanent way, but some of them in the third coach were trapped. Eventually, we got them all freed.

Following this more serious accident, the Board of Trade made an order that weights were to be placed underneath the seats of carriages to increase their stability during storms. The West Clare Railway then began to put heavy concrete slabs in practically all passenger vehicles. Those carrying the slabs were marked with a small white diamond-shaped sign at one end and during storms only carriages bearing this diamond sign were used for traffic.

Despite this precaution, a further alarming accident occurred just two years later. On Christmas Eve 1912 the 8.30 a.m. from Ennis headed by

Lahinch station, Co Clare at the end of the nineteenth century. Waves of the Atlantic ocean are clearly visible in the background.

4-6-0T engine No 1 Kilrush hauling a wagon, three carriages and a brake van was approaching Moy Bridge near Lahinch/*An Leacht*, when it became fully exposed to a south-westerly hurricane sweeping in from the Atlantic. The coupling between the engine and the first wagon broke and all the rolling stock toppled over along the side of the embankment. Although there was a fairly steep decline where the accident occurred, the vehicles fortunately did not roll to the bottom. There were only four people travelling on the train and thankfully there was no damage to life or limb. Following this further serious accident, the Board of Trade ordered that an anemometre be installed at Quilty station to record the velocity of the wind. It further ordered that trains were to use only ballasted vehicles when a gale reached 60 mph, but when the velocity of the wind reached 80 mph all traffic on the line was to be stopped.

Fierce storms continued to do considerable damage to the West Clare line throughout its existence, but no further incidents of trains being blown off the rails occurred after the installation of the anemometre at Quilty. Yet journeys on the line were undertaken with great care whenever Atlantic storms loomed and, right up until the final closure of this line in 1961, the Board of Trade strictures of 1912 were rigidly applied both by the Great Southern Railways and by Córas Iompair Éireann, successors to the former West Clare Railway who carried subsequent responsibility for the safety of travellers.

THE HARCOURT STREET ACCIDENT

Dublin at the end of the nineteenth century was a much different city from the cosmopolitan metropolis that today has assumed the confident air of a modern European capital. In 1900 Dublin was largely a run-down provincial city of the United Kingdom of Great Britain and Ireland, with a small colonial elite ruling an impoverished populace living mainly in squalid sub-standard housing and tenements that crowded the inner city. Employment was low-paid, mostly casual, and those fortunate enough 'to get a job on the railway' were considered to be well off, despite their deplorable conditions and inordinately long working hours.

In the first year of the twentieth century, on St. Valentine's Day 14 February 1900, a most spectacular railway accident happened at the Harcourt Street/*Sráid Fhearchair* terminus of the Dublin Wicklow & Wexford Railway (DW&WR) when a heavy cattle train from Enniscorthy failed to stop, crashed through the buffer stops and the outer station wall, leaving the engine perched precariously above Hatch Street some nine metres below. Miraculously nobody was killed but the driver of the train was trapped in the wreckage and had to have his right arm amputated.

Although the accident occurred 'at about 4.37 p.m. 14th inst.' according to the report of the Dublin Metropolitan Police (DMP), the story really begins more than twelve hours earlier in Enniscorthy, Co Wexford, where the crew of the ill-fated train booked on duty. The fireman, Peter Jackson, began work in the engine shed there at 4 a.m. and both the driver, William Hyland, and the guard, Robert Doran, joined him at 5 a.m. The cattle train of which they were in charge left Enniscorthy at 10 a.m. hauled by number 17 'Wicklow', an 0-6-0 engine fitted with an automatic vacuum brake in addition to the usual coal tender handbrake. It was significant that, apart from a halt at Gorey during which they had some breakfast, the crew had not been allowed any break for a meal throughout their working day.

On leaving Enniscorthy the train travelled north towards Dublin picking up wagon-loads of cattle from Gorey and Arklow, where a large number of beasts were collected from the local fair. The train finally loaded to thirty wagons, consisting of a leading timber wagon, twenty-eight cattle wagons and a guard's brake van at the rear. On the final stretch of the journey, one wagon was detatched at Foxrock and the heavy train then climbed up to the summit of the Harcourt Street line at Lakelands near Stillorgan, Co Dublin. Here steam was shut off and the cattle train was allowed to roll downhill on the continuously falling gradient towards the terminus at Harcourt Street. Having passed Dundrum, the driver applied the handbrake to the tender wheels and the guard applied his handbrake in the rear van. Approaching the terminus, however, the driver encountered difficulty in trying to bring his train to a halt. According to the report of the DMP, filed on 15 February 1900, the railway officials believed 'that the slippery state of the wheels and rails from the frost prevented the brakes from working efficiently'.

On realising that the handbrake fully applied to the coal tender's wheels would not be sufficient to stop the train at the terminus, the driver applied the vacuum brake. He then put the engine into reverse gear and finally turned on full steam but to no avail, as with the momentum generated by its heavy load the train could not stop. It continued through the station at a rapidly reducing speed, but crashed the buffer stops and ploughed through the metre-thick outer wall of the station. Masonry tumbled down on to Hatch Street some nine metres below, but the only casualty was a stationary furniture removal wagon owned by Messrs Pickford & Company which was broken by parts of the falling masonry. The DMP report added: 'The horse was also injured, but it is thought not seriously.'

Fortunately neither the fireman, guard, cattlemen, their beasts nor anyone on the street below were injured, apart from the horse. The fireman had jumped clear just before the impact, but the driver William Hyland who remained at his post was trapped by his right arm between the engine and its coal tender. The tender had fallen backwards from the outer wall into the pit separating it from the buffer stops, where it lay on its end together with the leading timber wagon. Before the unfortunate driver could be extricated from the wreckage, his right arm had to be amputated below the shoulder.

Engine number 17 'Wicklow' remained in the elevated position above Hatch Street for twelve days, while scaffolding was erected around it and plans made for its return to the railway. The amazing sight of the train engine perched above the street attracted large numbers of spectators, as well as many early photographers who captured for posterity views of this spectacular and historic Harcourt Street accident. Finally, on 26 February, number 17 was lowered by a twenty-ton crane to the ground in Hatch Street and, according to the DMP report 'from there it was recovered on the night

The crashed engine above Hatch Street on 14 February 1900.

of 27inst by men in the employment of Mr Spence, Civil Engineer of Cork Street. The men were engaged in the removal from 12 midnight until 4 a.m. 28th inst.' To ease the engine's return to the railway a temporary track was laid along the street to Earlsfort Terrace and around the corner into Adelaide Road as far as the ramp that led up to the goods yard at the eastern side of Harcourt Street station, where number 17 was finally re-railed.

The Board of Trade Report

An Investigating Officer from the Board of Trade, Colonel von Donop, was appointed in due course to investigate and report on the accident. He established that all three crew members of the ill-fated train had been on duty for some twelve hours when the accident happened and had not been allowed any interval for a meal break. According to the evidence presented at the inquiry the driver, William Hyland, had shut off steam at the top of Dundrum bank, where the handbrakes of both the tender and the rear van had been applied. The guard, Robert Doran, stated that he was of the opinion that the train was travelling too fast and Driver Hyland admitted that he had to use the vacuum brake to keep the train under proper control.

Both men stated, however, that the speed was moderate passing Milltown station almost two miles from the terminus, but Colonel von Donop maintained that if the speed there was moderate, no difficulty should have been experienced in halting the train. He concluded that the train was allowed to descend the Dundrum incline at rather a high rate of speed and found that Driver Hyland 'must have entirely misjudged his speed on entering the station'. Colonel von Donop pointed to the DW&WR Rule, which decreed that handbrakes only were to be used for controlling trains entering terminal stations. This clearly was not adhered to and evidence had pointed to its being habitually disregarded by drivers. At termini like Harcourt Street such observance was essential and Colonel von Donop advised that steps be taken by the company forthwith to ensure invariable compliance in future.

The Investigating Officer was also highly critical of the DW&WR on a number of counts. The buffer stops had clearly been wanting in strength and the fact that they were immediately preceded by a flexible turntable prevented the weight of the engine being used to hold the buffer stops in position, as would normally happen. Colonel von Donop stated that as these stops abutted on a public road at a considerably higher level, the situation was one where very strong stops should have been provided. The nearness of the turntable to the buffer stops was criticised and the report recommended that means be found to dispense with it and bring the buffer stops forward to a position where stronger stays could be provided to take the strain of any such future incident.

The Investigating Officer also advised the company that it would be very desirable to provide a direct connection from the main line into the goods yard to the east of the terminus. Such a connection would avoid having to bring all incoming goods trains into the buffer stops of the passenger platform and then having to shunt out again in order to reach the goods yard. The arrangements then existing 'would be unsuitable anywhere, but more especially so at Harcourt Street'. While work was being carried out on the desired alterations, Colonel von Donop recommended that, with a view to preventing goods trains entering Harcourt Street station at excessive speed, all such trains should be obliged to stop at an outer signal or else at Ranelagh, the previous station. A requirement of this kind would ensure that all drivers would have their trains well under control after descending the Dundrum incline and prior to entering the terminus. Concluding his report Colonel von Donop repeated that, while the accident was primarily due to a miscalculation of speed on the part of the driver, the faulty arrangements at the station 'must also be clearly regarded as having largely contributed to it'.

The Consequences

Smarting from this critical report, the DW&WR proceeded to implement its recommendations, but only to a limited extent. The turntable was left undisturbed, but the end wall and buffer stops were reconstructed and considerably strengthened. A very strong monolithic bastion to the buffer frame was built and hydraulic buffer stops were fitted. These proved their worth in later years when vehicles collided with the stops. At the south-eastern end of the station a direct connection to the goods yard was provided for incoming trains but, more significantly, a regulation was introduced requiring goods trains to stop at the previous station. This major consequence of the 1900 Harcourt Street accident became a permanent requirement and was soon made applicable to all classes of trains. Thus, right up to the final closure of the Harcourt Street line in 1958, all incoming trains had to stop at the previous station, Ranelagh.

It is interesting to trace the subsequent careers of the crew of the ill-fated Enniscorthy cattle train of 14 February 1900. William Hyland, the 22-year-old driver badly injured in the accident, spent a number of weeks in hospital before returning to his home in Bray, Co Wicklow. The loss of his right arm at such an early age was tragic and meant the end of his career on an engine footplate. To its credit, the DW&WR found him a post in the Locomotive Foreman's office at Bray Depot, where he was a familiar figure for many years. He lived to the age of 53, passing away on 1 February 1930. Peter Jackson, the fireman who jumped off before the crash happened, failed to report for duty on the day following the accident and was dismissed from service. He later secured a post in the Northern Power Station at Amiens Street Dublin, where he was employed for some years before emmigrating to England. Robert Doran, the guard of the cattle train, passed away at the early age of 40 on 26 November 1928. A son, Inspector Jack Doran, was employed by Córas Iompair Éireann (CIÉ) for many years at Westland Row station in Dublin, as well as at other locations.

The principal character of the spectacular accident at Harcourt Street on St Valentine's Day 1900, engine number 17 'Wicklow', ran for many further years on the south-eastern lines. It was rebuilt by the Dublin & South Eastern Railway, successor to the DW&WR, in 1920 and fitted with a larger boiler, but lost its name in the process. However, this unlucky engine was the victim of further incidents during the Civil War in Co Wexford in 1922-23. It was derailed at Killurin in July 1922 and was tumbled down Ballyanne bank in January 1923. But the brave engine recovered and was renumbered 440 in the railway amalgamation of 1925 by the Great Southern Railways (GSR). It ran for a further four years before finally being withdrawn from service and scrapped in 1929.

THE GOAT AT CASTLEREA

Some four miles south of Castlerea/*An Caisleán Riabhach* in Co Roscommon is a minor country road that crosses the Athlone to Westport railway by a level crossing at Frenchlawn. In the early hours of the morning of 11 April 1903, this was the scene of a serious accident that was renowned because it was alleged to have been caused by a goat.

The consequences were most serious as one passenger was killed and fifteen others injured when the Mayo night mail train ploughed into an obstruction on the line, which turned out to be a platelayers' trolley used by  workmen repairing the track. Immediate local investigations suggested that a goat was responsible for causing the trolley to have been on the mainline in the middle of the night four miles south of the station. People remembered that the local permanent way ganger was in the habit of tethering his goat to the axle of the trolley when it was left overnight on a siding in Castlerea. Popular wisdom had concluded that the goat must have moved off in the evening in search of new pastures pulling the trolley behind him and that gravity, combined with the hunger of the goat, caused the trolley to roll along the mainline as far as Frenchlawn.

However, when the Board of Trade appointed Colonel von Donop to hold a formal inquiry into the cause of the accident, he expressed grave doubts about the possibility of a goat being able or willing to pull a trolley that far in the middle of the night. The Colonel formed a theory that the trolley had been borrowed by locals to provide free transport home from a night's drinking session in Castlerea. But residents of Castlerea strongly resented and rejected that theory, pointing out that nothing was ever proven to substantiate it. Of course, it should also be recorded that no trace was ever found of the errant goat!

TRACK INSPECTION CYCLES

To maintain high safety standards, it was essential continually to inspect the railway track. Inspection vehicles were first introduced in America and were soon adopted by European railway systems. The track inspection cycle shown in the accompanying photograph was operating near Whitehead/*An Cionn Bán* in Co Antrim on the Belfast & Northern Counties Railway early in the twentieth century and was used by Permanent Way Inspectors on their regular rounds. Strict rules were enforced for these machines. Where there was double track, the inspecting cycle had to travel 'on the wrong line' so that its crew could see approaching trains in time to get their cycle off the track. Where there was only a single track, a thorough knowledge of the timetable was essential.

Track inspecting cycles can be driven at 30 mph on a falling gradient, 15 to 20 mph on the level and can easily be worked up a gradient of 1 in 30. In the *Appendix to the Working Timetable* published by the Great Southern Railways in 1935 comprehensive instructions were given to staff with regard to the use of inspection rail cycles. Great care and vigilance was urged and, in case of emergency, the cycle had to be abandoned rather than any personal risk be taken in attempting to save it. The cycle was not to be ridden round sharp curves where the view in either direction was bad, nor was it to be used after dusk, before daybreak or in a fog. Neither was it ever to be ridden through a tunnel. Then follow two interesting instructions, arising directly out of incidents that almost led to serious accidents:

> The persons using the cycle must make definite arrangements with each other as to which side of the line the cycle will be taken off in case of a train or engine coming unexpectedly.
>
> A padlock and chain must be carried with each cycle for the purpose of locking it when left at an out station or elsewhere for any length of time without a man in charge.

Track inspection cycle nearing Whitehead, Co Antrim in the 1890s.

Had the latter instruction been in force in 1903 it would have prevented the incident involving the goat at Castlerea that had never been traced!

Nowadays track inspection cycles have been largely superceded by motorised inspection cars.

PART TWO

CIVIL WAR SABOTAGE

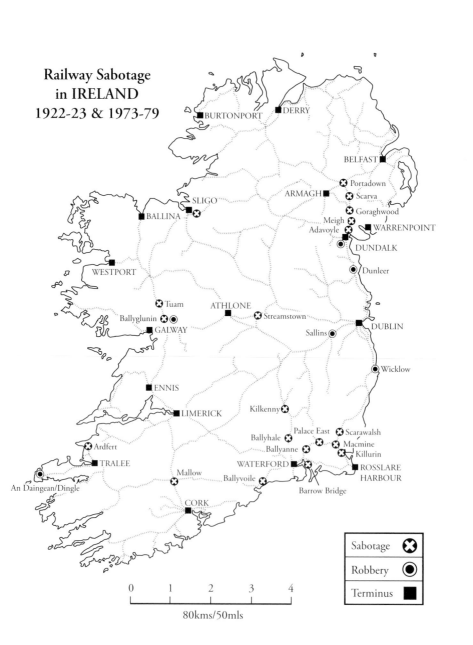

Railway Sabotage
in IRELAND
1922-23 & 1973-79

BURTONPORT
DERRY
BELFAST
Portadown
ARMAGH
Scarva
SLIGO
Goraghwood
BALLINA
Meigh
WARRENPOINT
Adavoyle
DUNDALK
WESTPORT
Dunleer
Tuam
ATHLONE
Ballyglunin
Streamstown
GALWAY
DUBLIN
Sallins
Wicklow
ENNIS
Kilkenny
LIMERICK
Palace East
Scarawalsh
Ballyhale
Macmine
Ardfert
Ballyanne
Killurin
WATERFORD
ROSSLARE
TRALEE
Mallow
HARBOUR
An Daingean/Dingle
Ballyvoile
Barrow Bridge
CORK

Sabotage
Robbery
Terminus

0   1   2   3   4

80kms/50mls

INTRODUCTION

Fear of alienating public opinion was probably the principal reason why significant destructive action was not taken against the railways during the Irish struggle for independence from the Easter Rising of 1916 until the signing of the Anglo-Irish Treaty in December 1921. There was no such restraint shown during the Irish Civil War of 1922-23, when disaffected republican fighters violently vented their anger against the new Irish Free State government which they accused of betrayal for accepting the Treaty that provided independence for only twenty-six of the thirty-two counties of Ireland.

As the new native government began to assert its authority from the end of June 1922, the anti-Treaty forces began to attack the railways in order to block the movement of the pro-Treaty government troops and their supplies to the south and west of Ireland. During the second half of 1922, particularly heavy damage was inflicted on the railways in south Tipperary, the Dundalk region and the Silvermines area of Co Tipperary, all key strategic communication areas. Rail communications in Co Kerry and in the far west of Counties Galway and Mayo were reduced to a bare minimum in this period. But with the intensification of action by pro-Treaty troops against them, the anti-Treaty forces decided in December 1922 on a policy for 'bringing the railways to a standstill, as on this to a great extent depends our campaign'. The purpose of their campaign was to prevent the functioning of the new government.

Although most of the destructive action taken against the railways in 1922-23 was sporadic and uncoordinated, it was nevertheless considerable. The Great Southern & Western Railway released details in January 1923 of the extent to which their property had been damaged during the previous year. Their report revealed that their lines had been damaged in 375 places, 42 engines had been derailed, 51 overbridges had been destroyed, together with 207 underbridges, 87 signal cabins and 13 other buildings. This scale of

Armoured cars of the Railroad Protection & Maintenance Corps at Glanmire Road station, Cork, 1923.

destruction inflicted on just one of the larger railway companies at that time was justified by the Chief of Staff of the anti-Treaty forces when he reminded his colleagues that, 'A hundred bridges blown up is just as effective a blow as a hundred barracks blown up.'

To try and effect repairs to the railway system and to protect railway workers, the government established the Railroad Protection & Maintenance Corps in October 1922. This corps was largely made up of railway workers and navies, who were paid at very favourable rates. Units of the corps were sent out to specific problem areas, beginning with the Clonmel-Thurles line and followed by lines in Co Cork. Duties of the corps were later developed to include the building of blockhouses at all important bridges, signal cabins and stations. At the works of the Great Southern & Western Railway at Inchicore in Dublin some 50 Lancia armoured cars were converted with flanged wheels to run on the railways. These were declared a great success as they could achieve a forward speed of 45 mph and a remarkable rearward speed of 20 mph. Some of these armoured cars were fitted with machine-gun turrets and were capable of carrying up to nine men.

By 1923 use was being made of improvised armoured trains, some consisting of Lancia cars attached to the roofs of railway carriages and fitted with swivel turrets to enable machine-gunners to fire in all directions. These trains were designed at Inchicore Works and were subsequently based at Cork, Limerick, Thurles and Clonmel. On the Midland & Great Western system the formidable *Queen of Connacht* was based at Mullingar to deal mainly with security problems in Co Westmeath. Another of these armoured trains, built in the Grand Canal Street works of the Dublin & South Eastern Railway (D&SER), was commandeered by the government in April 1923 for use on the Mallow-Killarney-Tralee line where serious attacks were taking place. It consisted of D&SER 2-4-2T engine No 64 fitted with armour-plating and placed in the middle of the train, preceded by a converted cattle wagon equipped with a search-light and machine guns. This in turn was preceded by a flat wagon loaded with concrete slabs, which was used to detect any booby-trap bombs placed on the line ahead of the train by anti-Treaty forces. Behind the armoured engine were further vehicles similarly equipped. The name *Faugh-a-Ballagh* (meaning 'Make Way!' in the Irish language) was painted on both sides of the engine. This armoured train returned to Dublin after some months, but permission was not given for the train to be dismantled until hostilities finally ceased in October 1923.

The Railroad Protection & Maintenance Corps scored many successes in reopening damaged railway lines and won much praise in Dáil Éireann, where one deputy said that the units had saved the country millions of pounds. But officers in charge of the many units of the corps were critical of the support they received from military commands. Local civic leaders also complained of delays before units of the corps would arrive to restore rail services in their areas. Particularly bad problems arose during the early months of 1923 in Counties Wexford, Sligo and Westmeath, where inordinate damage was caused to trains and railway property. Some of the more spectacular rail mishaps of the Civil War period are described in this part of the book.

THE DESTRUCTION OF
MALLOW VIADUCT

In the deliberate destruction of the railways during the Civil War of 1922-23, no single act caused so much hardship and loss to businesses and the wider community as the destruction of Mallow Viaduct on 9 August 1922. This railway bridge carried the double-track Dublin-Cork main line of the Great Southern & Western Railway across the River Blackwater just south of Mallow/*Magh Ealla* station in Co Cork. It was a magnificent cut-stone structure that consisted of ten twenty-metre arches built in 1848-49 for the opening of this principal artery of communication to the south of Ireland. The force of the high explosives used by the anti-Treaty forces caused not only the immediate destruction of the three northern arches, but also of the remaining seven arches that collapsed shortly afterwards resulting in the total destruction of the viaduct.

The original stone viaduct over the River Blackwater at Mallow, prior to its total destruction in August 1922.

With the ceremony over, guests adjourned to Moran's Hotel for luncheon, at which tributes were paid to the Great Southern & Western Railway, to the Railway Protection Corps and to Professor Crowley, a native of the Mallow region and one of the consulting engineers who had observed the work on behalf of the State.

With a continuous main line now restored between Dublin and Cork, a new timetable better suited to the public's needs was introduced and it included an improved service for mails. The *Cork Examiner* recalled with relief the hardships now past, which had resulted from the destruction of the viaduct and its detrimental effect on the trade of Cork. The newspaper continued:

> All travellers, who have had to negotiate the gap between 'Mallow South' and 'Mallow North' frequently, will long remember the rush and general confusion and the incidental expenses. But that was nothing as compared to the loss occasioned by the impossibility of sending goods and cattle direct.

Throughout the construction period of the new viaduct, which lasted from August 1922 to October 1923, all Cork goods and cattle traffic had to be handled by sea.

WAITING FOR AN AMBUSH

Ernie O'Malley was a medical student in Dublin when the Easter Rising of 1916 broke out. At first he was indifferent. But with the failure of the Rising, the executions and the aftermath, his feelings changed. He joined the Irish Volunteers, later to become the Irish Republican Army, and organised battalions and companies around Ireland. His abilities and outstanding personal courage led to his appointment as Officer Commanding, Second Southern Division. In the 1930s he wrote the classic book *On Another Man's Wound* which he himself described as an attempt to show the background of the struggle from 1916 to 1921 between an empire and an unarmed people. More than any other book of the period, it captures the essence of Ireland at the time.

Ernie O'Malley beautifully describes the location of a planned ambush of a train in North Cork in the autumn of 1920:

Jerry Kieley and I were on our way to the hills beyond the Blackwater. I was trying to get to a council of the North Cork Brigade in time. We had walked for a long time across low hills where branches of purple dogwood and crimson fuchsia hedges stood out against pale corn stubble and yellow hazel leaves. We crushed mauve heather and smelt the fragrance of yellow furze and bog myrtle; higher up were feathery green rowans behind their coral-red berries. It was a clear still day…

Near Millstreet we lay near a cutting to watch a train go by. We meant to attack a train when we would be told there were troops on board, but we did not get word that day. We heard like a great heart the rhythmic threshing stab of the piston and saw the snappy white blast. A moving train was always exciting as it shoved its way into space and time. The shining rail arteries connected me with my other life in Dublin, and the men perhaps with nearer memories, the platform excitement of a country town when 'Here she is' meant the daily paper and eager glances at the people who would again pull out of their lives. Cheered by the sight of the train we returned to field work.'

WAR IN COUNTY WEXFORD

Shortly after the outbreak of the Civil War at the end of June 1922, a South Eastern Division of anti-Treaty forces was formed in Co Wexford to operate as guerillas in open country rather than in towns. The town of Wexford was held by the pro-Treaty government troops throughout the Civil War period. At the beginning of the war, however, Waterford city was occupied by anti-Treaty forces but was taken by government troops with relative ease on 21 July 1922.

The guerilla assault on the railways began as a recognisable strategic plan to isolate Waterford from rail attack by government troops. Three lines radiating from the city were destroyed. Taylorstown Viaduct on the Rosslare-Waterford line, Bridge 457 between New Ross and Waterford, and the main line from Kilkenny were all blown up early in July 1922. But following the evacuation of Waterford by anti-Treaty forces on 21 July, the objective of the assault changed to become one of attacking soldiers on the move and disrupting the transport system of the country.

The war on the railways was nominally directed by the Higher Command of the anti-Treaty forces, but the Commmand was scarcely ever in control of field operations. However, general directives were issued such as:

- to interrupt the railways by every possible means;
- to destroy rolling stock;
- to ensure that stone houses capable of being fortified should not fall into the hands of government troops.

These directives were transmitted to the South Eastern Division Adjutant, whose headquarters were at Dunmain. The orders were discussed by a Brigade Council meeting in some central location, such as Palace or Taghmon. Women messengers were then used to relay the agreed orders to Section Leaders 'in the hope that something might happen', according to the

Waterford central signal cabin before it was burned down in November 1922.

All that remained of Waterford central signal cabin following sabotage by anti-Treaty forces.

evidence of survivors. Everything was left to the enterprise, skill, ingenuity and will-to-fight of each individual area. One former activist, Sketch White, both an engine driver and an insurgent, said that each active column worked on its own initiative and 'to that extent they were responsible to nobody'. Destructive activities were, therefore, sporadic in Co Wexford and were confined to areas haunted by small bands of zealots.

In the field, operating units were organised into flying columns detailed to carry out destructive tasks and then immediately scatter in all directions. They operated in four sections in Co Wexford: north from Enniscorthy; south from Murrinstown; central from Kyle; and west from New Ross. Each section consisted of a dozen or a score of men recruited from the zealots. When a man joined a column, he dedicated his life to the war. He became a marked man. There was no going back. Yet at the outposts, as in the Higher Command, there were differences in enthusiasm for the war on railways. Some advocated extreme measures, others moderation. It was often argued that the nation would need the railways again when the war was over. The railwaymen were shocked at the result of the explosion at Taylorstown Viaduct, which put the Rosslare-Waterford line out of commission for a year-and-a-half. All knew that very little more of such destructive action would close down the whole railway system and destroy a way of life. Destruction in Co Wexford could have been very much worse during the Civil War, but the fear of causing irreparable damage to railway livelihoods placed some form of restraint even on the zealots' plans.

Much of the account of the following incidents in Co Wexford has been based on interviews recorded by the late Dr George Hadden of Wexford in the 1940s and 1950s with many survivors of the Civil War period. The railwaymen's viewpoints are well reflected in the interviews with Michael Forde, Permanent Way Inspector with the Dublin & South Eastern Railway in Wexford and the opposite viewpoint in interviews with Dr Peadar Sinnott and Michael Flusk. Sketch White reflects both viewpoints. The other main source T. D. Sinnott, Brigadier in the War of Independence and in the Civil War, was described by Dr Hadden as 'a very much perturbed neutral with many friends on both sides'.

THE CAMPAIGN IN KILLURIN

Six miles north of Wexford/ *Loch Garman* station, on the banks of the River Slaney, nestles Killurin/ *Cill Liúrainn* station where the Carrigmannan ridge abuts into the river in rocky cliffs. Along either side of the ridge small steep glens make their way down to the river. Skirting the river at a general height of some 10-12m the railway makes its way by ledge and tunnel around the face of the cliffs and on by an embankment and bridge across the glen and county road to the continuing hills beyond. Where the embankment merges with the shoulder of the hills is perched Killurin station, walled like a little fort commanding both river and glen.

Sketch White, interviewed by Dr George Hadden in the early 1950s, said Killurin 'was in every way a handy place for an ambush'. As a station it had all the machinery for stopping trains. It stood isolated on its hills and a single armed man could occupy it effectively. A small band on the rising ground behind with its wonderfully good cover of fences and little woods could dominate the embankment. For miles below the station the railway skirts the river, almost as if made for wrecking. In the matter of escape routes, 'the first essential of all well-planned ambuscades,' according to Sketch White, there are plenty of little laneways and odd forgotten roads, while cross-country the whole area is full of unexpected little streams and patches of bog. 'Finally,' says Sketch, 'and this is important, the people were friendly.'

On 10 July 1922 members of the Kyle Column blew up a three-metre brick arch of Bridge 399 some sixty-five metres on the Wexford side of Killurin station. The span carried the railway over the little lane leading down to Killurin Quay. The bridge was broken without warning, the signals were set at clear and the lives of the engine crew of the 4.15 a.m. Wexford-Waterford goods train were thrown into great danger. The train was hauled by engine No 17, the same 0-6-0 engine that featured in the spectacular crash at Harcourt Street Dublin on St Valentine's Day 1900, and was crewed by Driver Mick Conway and Fireman Thomas Lee. The railroad was broken

Killurin station, Co Wexford. The gable-end window was used to overlook the embankment and all approaches to the station.

about seven metres short of the wrecked bridge but, in some extraordinary fashion, the engine travelling pretty fast managed to jump the three-metre gap. Driver Conway was steaming at the time and this may have helped the engine to clamber on to the sleepers on the far side. The engine took its tender across and came to rest at right angles to the railway, about its own length beyond the gap and lying completely outside the rails on the landward side, with the left leading wheel overhanging the bank. The first wagon behind the tender failed to make the jump and fell stern first into the gap. But the coupling held and, by anchoring the engine, it may have just saved it from toppling down the bank. Had the engine gone down, the crew could scarcely have escaped with their lives.

The Dublin & South Eastern Railway (D&SER) in the Wexford area were very fortunate in having at that time a loyal and courageous Permanent Way Inspector, Michael Forde, whose initiative, resource and energy ensured that the railways in his area continued to operate throughout the tempestuous Civil War period. When news of the incident at Killurin was telephoned to Wexford, Inspector Forde responded immediately and his breakdown gang had reached the scene of the wreck by 7.30 a.m. that morning. According to Michael Forde in an interview with Dr Hadden, their first task was to secure the engine by building a crib of sleepers under the overhanging wheel. Then, leaving the engine to Michael Cross, foreman of the Locomotive Department, Inspector Forde set about re-railing the wagons. He broke the railroad some distance behind the wreck and relaid it with flange rails out towards the scattered wagons. Then with the aid of a long chain the breakdown engine pulled the wagons one by one back on to the line. The wagon lying in the gap was jacked-up from below. The gang made good the gap with an emergency bridge of timber baulks, laid a pair of rails under the jacked-up engine, broke the railroad again and pulled it over to join up with the engine rails. Then the breakdown engine hauled No 17 back on to the main line. By 10.30 p.m. that night, the railway line had been restored and opened for traffic.

There was an interesting sequel to this event in 1935. Thirteen years after the incident at Killurin, Driver Mick Conway at the age of 51 was being compulsorily retired on medical grounds as he was going deaf. All appeals to the Great Southern Railways, as successors to the Dublin & South Eastern Railway, had failed and his friends and colleagues put forward a case in court that the deafness was a result of the shock of his experience early that July morning in Killurin. The case was heard before Judge M. Comyn in Wexford. Inspector Forde handed into court his own photographs of the 1922 wreck and was able 'to swear honest and fair that, travelling with Mick Conway on the footplate, I used to be able to talk with him as with any other man'. Having heard the case, the judge asked 'Is there anybody here who can speak for the company? I can decide the case now, but I'd like to wait to hear what the company is going to do about it.' The very next morning, a telegram was received from the company offering Mick Conway the post of steam-raiser at Tramore, Co Waterford, where he continued to work until his retirement on pension in 1949.

Inspector Michael Forde (in bowler hat at the front) supervises the recovery of engine No 36, which was deliberately run off the rails on 14 October 1922.

The Ambush of 24 July 1922

Just two weeks after the wrecking of Bridge 399, the Wexford Mail was ambushed at Killurin. When station master Philip Fox, as was his custom, came on to the platform at 4.30 p.m. on the afternoon of 24 July to watch the Mail go through at speed, he was surprised to see ten to twelve armed men running towards him. While the rest ran on, one stayed behind at the station and forced the station master to put the signals at danger. Then he demanded the red flag, locked Philip Fox in his office, threw the key on the platform and went to fix the red flag between the rails some 30 metres on the Wexford side of the station.

Half an hour earlier in Wexford forty prisoners had been put on the Mail train under an escort of forty-six soldiers in charge of Lieutenant P. Leonard. The escort occupied the first and third coaches, the prisoners the second. In the rear coach were twenty-five unarmed recruits under Captain Myley Redmond. The rest of the train was crowded in every compartment with ordinary passengers. That day the guard did not report for duty, but sent word that he had sprained his ankle. Sketch White was the engine driver and with him on the footplate was the Permanent Way Inspector, Michael Forde.

T. D. Sinnott, a friend of the late Dr George Hadden, was travelling from Wexford by that train. At the station he joined up with a worthy citizen of Enniscorthy who was also travelling. They had just bought their tickets when the station master approached T. D. Sinnott privately and said in a very low voice, 'You're not to travel on that train.' 'Why, what's wrong with it?' protested Sinnott. 'There's nothing wrong with it,' replied the station master, 'I was told to tell you and that ought to be good enough for you.' It was. T. D. Sinnott turned to his travelling companion and suggested that they have a drink across the road at the Imperial before the train left. 'But have we the time?' asked his friend. 'Lots of time and anyhow they'll hold her a few minutes for me,' was the reply. So off they went for their drink and off went the train without them, to the great anger of the worthy citizen of Enniscorthy. But forever after when they met again, his friend would say to Sinnott, 'Wasn't it the lucky thing we missed that train.'

The Mail Train left Wexford on time and after passing Killurin Tunnel it slowed down to cross the temporary Bridge 399 just outside the station. Just as the train overran the red flag, the firing started from the rising ground above the station. Some 30 metres further on the engine was just within the cover of the three-metre brick wall of the station, but the rest of the train was strung out in the open on the embankment. The train stopped with all brakes on and Sketch White shouted across the footplate to Inspector Forde that there was a rail dislodged ahead. The firing, coming from behind a hedge about 50 metres away, was concentrated on the first and third coaches.

The escort of soldiers clambered down on to the permanent way and, sheltering behind the wheels, returned the fire. The prisoners were lying on the floor of the second coach and praying to be let out. Lieutenant Leonard came up to the engine and ordered the driver to draw the train on into the shelter of the station wall. Sketch White replied that his brakes were jammed. Meanwhile Inspector Forde ran up the platform looking for the station master. He found the key on the platform, released him and then telephoned to Wexford and Enniscorthy that the Mail was being ambushed and to send ambulances for three badly wounded men. In the event, all three died. The military escort by now had occupied Killurin station and were developing a dangerous encircling movement to take the ambuscade in the rear. So the Kyle Column, having failed to panic the escort or to rescue the prisoners, withdrew and scattered. Within twenty-five minutes of the first shots, firing ceased and all was calm.

When the train moved on, a number of army officers rode on the engine. There proved to be nothing wrong with the brakes and no rails had been dislodged ahead. A mile beyond Killurin a platelayers' bogie had been abandoned on the line by the attackers after they had commandeered it from its crew of linesmen returning from an inspection of the line. The delayed Wexford Mail reached Macmine Junction one hour behind time, where it stopped to cross the mixed train from Enniscorthy in the charge of Driver Mike Hogan. He was all a gog for the latest news and he ran around the other train to talk to Sketch White on the Mail engine. He told Dr Hadden that he never reached that engine because of the sickening sight:

> The running boards of the leading coaches were a horror, with blood oozing out from under the doors. I went no further. I thought I'd never get back to my own engine to get sick.

When the Wexford Mail reached Enniscorthy, Driver Sketch White was taken off his engine and arrested for being in collusion with the ambuscade and therefore responsible for the death of three soldiers. Sketch was put into the coach with the other prisoners and that coach together with the two escort coaches was detached from the Mail, which was sent on its way some two hours late in the charge of Driver Tom Sutton. The three military coaches were made up as a special train that left later in the charge of Driver Christie Fortune of Bray. Mike Hogan, the driver of the Enniscorthy train that had crossed the Mail at Macmine Junction, was called out again as soon as he reached Wexford and sent back on engine No 25 to act as a pilot engine to precede the military special all the way through to Harcourt Street station in Dublin. An officer rode with him on the footplate. He told Dr Hadden:

> It was a nerve-racking job, looking before for obstructions and after to

keep contact with the special. But for that officer on the footplate, I would've made sure to lose the fellow behind and get away out of it all.

His instinct in sensing danger was right. Sketch White told Dr Hadden many years later that a wrecking party from Dalkey was coming up from Killiney as the special passed. 'They had missed her by minutes. Their instructions were to wreck her at Shanganagh Junction'.

At Harcourt Street station the train was ambushed for the second time. Mike Hogan told that he had just got his engine on to the turntable at the end of the platform when all hell broke loose. His panic instinct was to bolt, but his more experienced colleague on the turntable got him down and held him until he came to his senses. The noise of the firing in the vaulted station and the whiz of ricocheting bullets were terrifying. The attackers had come up the main stone stairs of the station from the street below and apparently did not debouch from there. Some firing was also coming from the open goods-yard end of the station, where get-away possibilities were excellent. Sketch White said that escort soldiers and prisoners lay flat. He heard the officer in command order, 'Point those rifles to the sky.' 'Otherwise,' Sketch added, 'they'd have been shooting one another.' Only the front ranks returned the fire and that lasted only a few minutes. 'A very short time,' said Sketch, 'as was normal in such attacks'. Then as suddenly as it had begun, the firing stopped and the attackers, fearing encirclement, withdrew. The prisoners were then taken in lorries to the gaols.

As usual, there was an interesting sequel to this adventure. The following week a Coroner's Jury meeting in Enniscorthy returned an open verdict as to Driver White's complicity in the death of the soldiers at Killurin. Six weeks later, at the initiative of the General Manager of the D&SER and at a cost of £63 for Counsel, Sketch was released under writ of *habeas corpus* issued by the company. He was one of the last to be so released. For about that time rights of *habeas corpus* were suspended under the Emergency Powers. In February 1923 Sketch White was again arrested under the Emergency Powers and held until the following October, long after the Civil War had come to an end.

Removed Rails in Killurin Tunnel
On 15 August 1922 two lengths of rail were removed just within the Wexford end of Killurin tunnel. There was no advance warning and the night mail goods train from Dublin, in charge of Driver George Turner and Fireman O'Brien of Bray, ran into the trap. The engine No 14 left the rails but continued to run on the sleepers for some 30 metres before it reached soft ground and turned over. The driver was pinned under the engine. Word

Sabotage of the Dublin-Wexford night goods train headed by engine No 14 at Killurin tunnel on 15 August 1922.

was telephoned to Wexford at 5.20 a.m. and Inspector Forde immediately sought a military ambulance and personally guided it to Killurin, just as Driver Turner was being extricated from the wreckage badly scalded. He was rushed to Wexford Hospital and was off work for a full year. However, he made a good recovery and subsequently served for many more years before retiring on pension.

The breakdown train arrived around 7.15 a.m. and Inspector Forde worked all day to try and re-rail twenty-two wagons, mostly of coal. This he achieved, despite the continuous pilfering of the train's cargo by the local people throughout the day. By 10.00 p.m. that night, all the wagons were back on the rails, but the Locomotive Department had great trouble in recovering engine No 14. Foreman Michael Cross had managed to jack up the engine to an angle of 45 degrees, but the ground fell away sharply outside it and he could not make further progress as the jacks slipped continually. Late in the evening a carpenter by the name of Maguire remembered, 'They've got an endless-chain block at Thompson's on the Quay. If we had that we'd pull her the rest of the way easy.' The pilot engine was sent to Wexford and returned within an hour with Thompson's endless-chain block.

They fixed the block to a tree across the line and at the first pull the engine came over on to its wheels. By 2.00 a.m. next morning they had rails under the engine. Then they re-laid the main line around the re-railed engine to allow the night goods from Wexford to get through. The next day, after the morning train from Dublin had passed, the breakdown gang returned, broke the railroad, joined it up with the rails under the wrecked engine and pulled it back on to the main line to be towed into Wexford. The main line was then re-laid and restored to its permanent alignment.

The Rushed Road Block

On 1 November 1922 the Wexford Mail was ambushed again at Killurin. The aim of the ambush was never clear, but Inspector Forde believed that a vanload of new bicycles being sent up daily from Pierce's in Wexford to the army in Dublin was the target. The ambush was laid near a ballast-pit about one kilometre north of Killurin, where the line rounded a blind curve. The engine was No 67 with Driver Sandy Hogan and Fireman Jack Rogan. Inspector Forde was on the footplate. He had just finished relaying that section of the line and wanted to test whether or not the train would sway at speed on the curve. Therefore, he had asked the driver to run the engine at a good 50mph as it came around the bend.

Suddenly, less than 100 metres ahead, they saw the road-block. It consisted of eight to ten sleepers built up impressively, but flimsily, to a height of about a metre with red flags flying from the corners. At the speed the engine was running it was too late to stop the train in that distance, even if the driver had kept his head. But Sandy was never at his best in an emergency. Now excited and confused he struck the road-block at a good 45mph, totally demolishing it in a cloud of steam. Then, having crashed the barrier and with Inspector Forde urging him to keep going at least until they were out of range, Sandy braked his engine to a stop some 500 metres further along the line in a cutting with a bridge overhead.

There happened to be two army officers on the train, Sandy Kavanagh and a lieutenant named Smith, both described as 'fire-eaters'. Immediately the train stopped, they jumped to the ground and drawing their revolvers went back down the line firing at the double as they went. The attackers, already demoralised by the wholly unexpected turn of events, now believed that they had stumbled on a military train and without waiting scattered. At the other end of the train the engine crew, listening to the noise of the battle, were crouching under cover of the tender believing themselves to be under fire. Then Dick Hammond, the ticket-checker, came up to them to ask what the feck they were waiting for. 'Them fellas,' he said, 'has run to Hell long ago.' So they climbed down and examined the engine to discover that one sleeper had penetrated the ashpan and another had jammed in the lifeguards.

The cylinder covers were broken and the draincocks snapped off. But No 67 could move and so they continued to Macmine Junction, where the engine of the train that had come from Waterford was borrowed to take the Wexford Mail through to Dublin.

Inspector Forde changed at Macmine Junction into the train going to Wexford, having had enough excitement for one day. He exchanged the footplate for a seat in an empty first-class carriage. But just before the train departed an army officer joined him, Commandant Gallagher OC of the Free State troops in Wexford, to ask what had happened on the way. 'Another ambush at Killurin,' replied Michael Forde. As the train was scheduled to stop at Killurin within the next fifteen minutes, it seemed entirely likely that the anti-Treaty attackers would be waiting for them to get a little of their own back. That suited Commandant Gallagher. He settled himself down beside Inspector Forde and placed a Mills bomb on either side of him. 'Look out,' he ordered as they came in sight of Killurin. ' See if they're waiting for us and give me a chance.' But to the Commandant's disgust and to the Inspector's undisguised relief, there was nobody there. The station staff asserted that they had seen the attackers going back and scattering.

A week later, in the Main Street of Wexford, a girl handed a note to Driver Sandy Hogan. It explained to him in detail what happened to men who tried to rush ambushes when they had been told to stop. Clearly it was calculated at least to upset, if not to intimidate him.

Engines in the River Slaney
On 11 November 1922, on the Wexford side of Killurin station, the rails were pulled out to the edge of the embankment above the River Slaney and were broken ahead of the night goods train from Dublin, hauled by engine No 18. This time the attackers stopped the train by signal and took the crew off, before driving the engine and its coal tender into the river at about 5.00 a.m. in the morning. Within half-an-hour word had reached Wexford and by 7.30 a.m. the breakdown gang was at the scene. Inspector Forde immediately deflected the main line around the wrecked train so that traffic could be kept moving again by 9.00 a.m. that same morning.

No 18 was a powerful engine, built in D&SER's own works in Grand Canal Street, Dublin. Now it had rolled down the river bank at Killurin like a boulder, rolling over and over, leaving deep marks on the bank but suffering little damage in the process. The engine lay on its side in the Slaney just below Killurin Quay. It posed a real problem for Permanent Way Inspector Michael Forde and Locomotive Department Foreman Michael Cross. Looking back, Michael Forde told the late Dr George Hadden, 'I've often wondered since how we managed it. She was sunk about half-way in the

Recovering engine No 18 at Killurin from the River Slaney, to which it was dispatched by anti-Treaty forces on 11 November 1922.

mud. At high tide she was completely under water.'

The recovery of No 18 from the River Slaney called for great resource and ingenuity at a time when heavy specialised lifting equipment was not available. The fascinating story of how it was achieved is told in the appendix, but suffice it to say here that four rafts built of sleepers had to be sunk into the river bed and from these the engine was jacked-up, rails placed under it and heavy anchor chains used to haul No18 up a ten-metre embankment and along the county road back to Killurin station.

Incredibly, just about two weeks later, another engine No 32 was similarly despatched to the River Slaney by the anti-Treaty attackers. It had been hauling the 9.15 p.m. night passenger train from Wexford to Waterford and had stopped at Macmine Junction to connect with the evening train from Dublin hauled by engine No 68. The attackers had come to the Junction to wreck the engine of the Dublin train, but when they discovered that No 68 was being driven by Sketch White they left his engine with him and took No 32 instead. Passengers and crew of the Waterford train were turned out on to the dismal platform of Macmine Junction, while their train was taken to Killurin for wrecking. It was late on a cold November evening and as the passengers were hungry at this isolated spot miles from the nearest shop, Sketch White did what he could to provide comfort for them. As well as inviting them into the carriages of the Dublin train, he provided hot steam to the heating-coils beneath the seats and hot water for those fortunate enough to have been prepared for tea-making throughout the night.

Meanwhile the wreckers had reached Killurin and, for some unknown reason, sent only the engine into the River Slaney leaving the carriages on the main line. The techniques of wrecking and of salving No 32 were identical to those of 11 November and No 32 soon took its place on the loading bank at Killurin immediately behind No 18. Both engines stood there over Christmas 1922 and then, on St Stephen's Day, the breakdown gang built a ramp with rails connected to those under the wrecked engines. Then they backed their own engine up to the bottom of the ramp, pushing before it five vacuum-fitted wagons which were coupled to the stricken engines and then reversed to lead them gently from the loading bank down to the rails.

As 1922 was drawing to a close, the role of Killurin as a strategic wrecking location had diminished. The Kyle Column still had to play a part in the burning of trains at Macmine Junction, but the centre for anti-Treaty activity definitely moved over towards the mountains. Sketch White explained the forsaking of Killurin as due to the tightening up of security measures in Co Wexford, particularly the tactic of encirclement. In open country with road access to all sides, that tactic proved a very dangerous operation for guerillas. It was less easy to apply it in the roadless skirts of the mountains.

KEEPING THE LOCALS FRIENDLY

Inspector Forde was frequently irritated by the behaviour of the country people in areas where his breakdown gang had to work during the Civil War. After the wrecking of the night goods train at Killurin Tunnel on 15 August 1922, he considered:

> The amount of pilfering they did was disgraceful. You couldn't watch 'em. They'd take anything. They came with horses and carts from far and near. On that particular goods train there was besides the twenty-two wagons of coal a consignment of tea and of drapery goods. For long enough afterwards, there was all the tea the countryside could use. I knew of one house in the area where they had 35 velour hats.

Inspector Forde agreed that property should not concern the breakdown gang. Then he added caustically:

> I had me own work to do. But if the senior officials of the company were disinclined to venture near a wreck – and that was notorious – I done me best. At least I collected up all parcels and movable property and got it off into safety.

There was, however, another viewpoint. Michael Flusk told Dr Hadden bleakly: 'Pilfering of the trains was no concern of ours. We did our job and left it so.' Sketch White expanded on this aspect of the case:

> It was the outsiders that did the real damage, the pilfering of the trains. But then, too, that did help to keep the local people friendly.

SINGLE-HANDED COUP

On the South Wexford line from Rosslare to Waterford is Ireland's longest railway river crossing, the Barrow Bridge near Campile/ *Ceann Poill* station. It is almost a mile in length and consists of twelve lattice steel girder sections, with a central opening section to facilitate shipping traffic upriver to and from New Ross. In February 1923 this substantial railway structure was effectively immobilised for a lengthy period by the imaginative action of one individual, who did not have to use any dynamite nor even a crowbar.

Young Peadar Sinnott borrowed a salmon cot and rowed out alone to the great bridge, where he landed on the footing frame of the opening span. He climbed up to the operation cabin where he unlocked the bridge and, using the small crown-wheel, swung the bridge open to shipping traffic. It was so simple, he said, that a child could have done it. Then, after removing a single nut, he lifted out the crown-pinion wheel and dropped it in the river. And he calmly rowed back to the shore.

It was only afterwards that he discovered there was a detachment of troops guarding the bridge. Had they seen him on the bridge or realised what he was doing, he wouldn't have had a chance in the world of getting back alive. For some time after, the Court Martial was busy apportioning blame. Looking back, Dr Sinnott told his medical colleague Dr Hadden that he really should have shown the engineers where he dropped the thing. 'They could have picked it up with an oyster-dredger.'

WRECKING TRAINS AT MACMINE

About ten miles north of Wexford was the isolated station of Macmine/*Maigh Maighin*. Situated on the marshy verges of the River Slaney, with neither a village, a bridge nor a ferry to support it, the station nevertheless played an important role in the daily operation of the Dublin & South Eastern Railway. From here a line to Waterford diverted westwards from the Dublin main line and this justified the isolated station's official title of Macmine Junction. Until its closure in 1963, the only road access was by way of a grassy lane from the county road about half-a-mile to the south-west. Macmine Junction was, therefore, at the end of a cul-de-sac, a dangerous trap for incautious attackers.

The station had three through lines. The main lines to and from Dublin, each with its own platform, and the Waterford line running at the back of the Dublin platform which was thereby transformed into an island platform. At both ends of the station were crossovers to connect the Waterford line both with the main line north to Enniscorthy and Dublin and south to Wexford and Rosslare. Under normal operational practice, northbound and southbound mainline trains were scheduled to cross each other at Macmine and make connections with trains to and from Waterford. Thus, at certain times of the day, Macmine Junction would present a very busy scene with three connecting passenger trains, as well as goods and special trains parked in sidings awaiting their turn to follow the priority passenger services.

Early in the Civil War, Macmine Junction became a primary target of destruction for the anti-Treaty forces. The tall signal cabin, commanding all three approaching lines and controlling all signals, telephones and switch points, was first attacked and burnt on 9 September 1922 but the attackers failed to put it out of commission. They returned with a vengeance on 3 January 1923, re-burnt the temporary signal cabin and went on to burn down all the station buildings used for the comfort of the passengers and staff, including the ticket office, waiting rooms and refreshment room. Why

Macmine Junction station with a train to Waterford at left and a mixed train from Enniscorthy to Wexford at right. The line to Dublin is behind the name board.

this was done, rather than wrecking the signalling and point-switching system, remains a mystery as their repeated destructive action failed to affect the operation of trains through Macmine Junction.

But a third and much more serious attack followed on 27 January 1923. A large party of some 35 to 40 attackers recruited from mixed columns throughout Co Wexford descended on Macmine Junction to ambush the Wexford Mail supposed, erroneously, to be carrying some 28 armed government troops. As in previous raids on the same train, the riverside embankment near Killurin station was chosen as the hold-up point. The railroad was broken in the station and pulled foul. In front of the break was placed a barrier of sleepers and under the cliffs beyond the embankment a 10-12lb mine connected by cable to an electric detonator was laid under the track, in case the train should try to reverse out of the trap. As in the Killurin ambush the previous July, the main group of attackers lay along a ditch on rising ground beyond the station dominating the embankment.

Across the River Slaney was a flanking detachment to deal with any troops who might take shelter on the river face of the embankment, while a further detachment was stationed along the Wexford road to command the Carrigmannan Viaduct and deal with any troop reinforcements sent by road. Lastly, to forestall the danger of troops establishing themselves in the little station-fortress of Killurin, Peadar Sinnott told Dr Hadden that he had established himself with a Thompson machine-gun in an armchair at an upper window in the gable-end of the station house, overlooking the embankment and all approaches to the station. Dr Hadden was told: 'My gun rested on a pillow on the window-sill. The station master was controlled with a revolver, but his wife supplied me with tea and cake.' Peadar Sinnott's lasting regret was that he never adequately thanked the good woman, the more so because when the firing started all the delicate vases in that room were shattered.

The Mail from Wexford arrived on time at 4.30 p.m. and, since it was not scheduled to stop at Killurin, the driver ignored the signals and precipitated immediate shooting. An ordinary passenger on the train Lieutenant Charles Burke was killed, Billy Mahony the engine fireman was shot through both legs and, in the mail van, a sorter named Fitzpatrick, while lying on the floor, felt a tap on his head and found that a bullet had gone through his cap. The expected troop contingent was not on the train, so the outposts of ambushers were recalled to the station by short blasts of the engine whistle. When all the ambushers had returned, they removed the obstruction ahead of the train, re-made the railroad and jumped aboard the train, which was then driven on to Macmine Junction some three miles to the north. According to one passenger on the train quoted in a local newspaper, *The Free Press*: 'One of their leaders wore a rosary of big mother-of-pearl beads round his neck.'

At Macmine Junction the passengers and crew of the trains already there who had been listening apprehensively to the noise of firing down-river at Killurin, were greatly relieved to see the Wexford Mail arrive. However, their relief soon turned to fear when they realised what was being planned. There were already four trains waiting at Macmine Junction. Two were in the sidings, an empty cattle special and a ballast train. The other two were on through lines: the mixed train from Enniscorthy at the riverside platform and the connecting train from Waterford on the inland side of the island platform. The Mail train from Wexford was brought in between the last two trains on the other side of the island platform. However, the raiders decided to run the Mail well beyond the platform until the engine, but not the coaches, fouled the crossover from the Waterford line. Then the raiders swarmed out and took control of Macmine Junction. They unhooked the engine No 67 and sent it off driverless towards Dublin to face an uncertain fate. Soon the astonished station master at Edermine Ferry to the north telephoned to say: 'She has just gone through here mad.' Then No 67 passed through Enniscorthy at speed and only came to rest finally when it ran out of steam beyond Camolin, a distance of 30 kilometres from Macmine!

Having got rid of the Wexford Mail engine, the anti-Treaty attackers turned their attention to the other four trains in the station. Their plan was to run the train from Waterford back through the crossover to the north of the station and on to the main line to Dublin. There it would meet the Enniscorthy train which would be run backwards into the northern crossover, so that both trains would jam and derail each other. The combined might of their respective engines under a full head of steam would crumple their carriages and pile them around the Mail train coaches left standing on the line between. All went according to plan with remarkable speed and efficiency. The attackers sent the Enniscorthy train about a mile out towards Wexford and then reversed it driverless back to the wrecking point with full momentum. The train from Waterford was similarly reversed from a standing start at the island platform and crashed into the reversing Enniscorthy train towards its end, just beyond the station platforms where both trains piled up as planned. Then the wreckers ran the empty cattle train from a long siding into the heap and finally drove the ballast train into the piled-up wreckage.

It was a frightening scene of total destruction witnessed by the evicted passengers huddled together in groups on the platforms. Having piled up the four trains, the anti-Treaty wreckers then poured petrol over them and set them alight. Then they hastily left Macmine Junction. Being very conscious of the station's dangerous location at the end of a cul-de-sac off the county road, they made their get-away along the Waterford line in the direction of New Ross in three separate groups, each with a machine-gun covering their retreat. At Sparrowsland they ascended Bree Hill from where they scattered and dispersed into the countryside.

By some oversight, the attackers had failed to cut the telephone wires and both Killurin and Macmine were in touch with Wexford throughout the raids. Although the military were notified almost immediately after the incidents, Inspector Forde was very critical that his breakdown gang were first to arrive at Macmine around 6 p.m. Dr Hadden was unable to establish a reason for the slow response of the military, but conceded that an assault on Bree Hill held by resolute men with machine-guns was not an enterprise to be lightly tackled!

When Inspector Michael Forde arrived at Macmine Junction there was little that could be done. The fires were dying down and the crews of the five

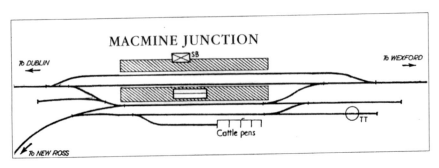

The wrecking took place on the crossovers at the Dublin end of the junction.

trains were setting out rather disconsolately to trudge home to Wexford, Enniscorthy or Waterford. The wreckage of the trains lay across all three through lines just beyond the Dublin end of the platforms. Little of those trains remained, except the wreckage of the Wexford Mail. All of the Enniscorthy train was destroyed except the guard's van and a horsebox at its extreme end. The engine had lost its dome, its chimney was twisted and 'its front was bent up as if it was made of cardboard'. According to Inspector Forde the Waterford train was burnt so completely that 'nothing remained to show that it had been a train, but some charred fragments and blackened wheels'. The wrecking plan had placed the Wexford Mail in the middle of the conflagration with wrecks piled on either side of it, but by some miracle it escaped with the least damage. While its four carriages including the dining car were largely saved by extinguishers, Inspector Forde said 'the Wexford Mail looked as if it had come through a siege. From end to end it was pitted with bullet holes, panels perforated and glass smashed.' But it still could move its wheels and on the following day, Sunday 24 July, the four surviving coaches were hauled through to Dublin.

The cost of the total damage caused at Macmine Junction to the Dublin & South Eastern Railway was estimated to have exceeded £50,000, an enormous sum at that time. To afflict such damage to no less than five trains in the short time at the attackers' disposal confirms that detailed planning and discipline of a high order were involved on the part of the anti-Treaty forces. Dr Hadden believed that even the metal parts of the trains were successfully destroyed and he recorded that the steel frames of some of the coaches were still lying in the long grass outside the station when Inspector Forde retired in 1944.

THE SCARAWALSH AMBUSH

This ambush was unique in its ruthlessness. The Civil War had reached a peak of bitterness during January 1923, when railwaymen and others were being killed in many parts of Ireland. From the evidence collected by Dr Hadden on the ambush at Scarawalsh north of Enniscorthy/*Inis Córthaigh*, it seems that Driver Sketch White and Fireman Jack Rogan were anxious to give their attackers the benefit of any possible doubt, but the facts are damning. The railway was broken at the actual site of the ambush and that reveals only an evil intent. The train was meant to crash there directly under the fire of the ambuscade.

The ambushed train was the 6.05 p.m. Rosslare Boat Train from Harcourt Street, Dublin. When ambushed on the night of 18 January 1923, it was 9.30 p.m. and pitch dark. There was no warning. The railway was broken by the crooked bridge over the River Bann at Solsborough. Sketch White, who was driving engine No 68, was travelling fast at the time when suddenly he saw a light immediately ahead 'as if it might be someone nervously lighting a cigarette'. He was emphatic that there was no reasonable warning. 'I grabbed the controls,' he said, 'shut off steam with one hand and with the other pulled the brake-lever full on – and that is a thing that is very seldom done. Nearly immediately we were off the road.' His fireman Jack Rogan had no doubts at all about the absence of warning:

> We always ran fast over that section. We were running at sixty miles an hour then. The night was pitch black and in those days engine crews had red lights on the brain. They'd see them in their sleep. But that night there were none. Sketch jammed on the brakes and almost immediately we were on the sleepers. Sketch had the wit to climb on to the tender. I myself and the pilot travelling with us that night were paralysed by the suddenness of it and the terrifying bursts of machine-gun fire. We couldn't stir. The tender was riding up on us. A couple more bumps and it'd have us flattened against the back of the boiler… We had a heavy

train behind us that night with six bogies: and all the makings of a first-class catastrophe. And it's lucky we were, every one of us, to come out of Scarawalsh that night alive.

As the train came to rest, there were shouts of 'Get out! Get out! Stick'em up! Surrender!' Sketch White said the firing came from the left of the engine, from behind a ditch. 'It was,' said Sketch, 'a most wonderful place for an ambush – I wish I'd found it myself – with dark hills back and front and a bog, almost like a moat, all round except at one spot. They were expecting a big number of troops on that train, though actually there was only a handful, a score or so, in all.' 'Which,' Peadar Sinnott told Dr Hadden years later, 'was evidence of shocking mismanagement. Anything so serious as the wrecking in full flight of a mainline passenger train deserves at least the confirmation of a telegram, which need only concern market produce or anything else with numbers in it.' What is quite certain is that, but for Sketch White's almost miraculously quick reaction, the smash would have been memorable in the records of the Civil War.

Sketch White said that when he applied the brakes: 'Everything in the tender came all over me.' Two carriages followed his engine off the rails and but for the retardation of the brakes all down the train 'and the application,' said Sketch, 'begins with the last coach,' the whole lot would have telescoped with all the added horrors of fire in the gas-lit carriages. As it was, nobody

A modern Rosslare-Dublin push-pull train in 1999 headed by diesel engine 071 at Scarawalsh where the ambush took place on 18 January 1923.

was hurt. Sketch White continued: 'Rogan was so hot at being wrecked without warning that he gave impudence to the raiders. So they dragged him off the engine and took him away. But they didn't harm him. I kept me mouth shut and they left me alone.'

The women were taken off the train and sent to Enniscorthy by cars held in readiness by the attackers. The men were required to walk. The soldiers on board the train were stripped to shirts and boots to provide future disguises for the anti-Treaty forces. The train was then doused in petrol and set on fire. 'It was first-class rolling stock, practically new,' said Sketch White. 'Why they'd be running their good stock in those times I wouldn't know.' But those bogie coaches ran no more, for after this ambush all bogie stock was put in store and even mainline trains were made up of old six-wheeled coaches. Within one minute of their being doused with petrol, the train coaches were a mass of flames. Nothing was left of them but the frames and wheels. The gas cylinders, two under each coach, added to the excitement by exploding one after the other as the fire reached them, to the consternation of the bystanders who scattered believing them to be grenades. The cost to the Dublin & South Eastern Railway of this episode was estimated to be £15,000 at that time.

A report in the *Wexford People* of 24 January 1923 noted that after the ambush at Scarawalsh the vans of the train were unhooked by the military and pushed back into safety. But the vans did not escape pillage. The newspaper reported: 'Around the vans parcels were strewn about, most of them open. Many had only the wrappings left.' Sketch White told Dr Hadden: 'There were eleven post-bags all ripped up for what they might contain. That time it was the soldiers that did it. I watched them and I reported to our manager by telephone. He told me they knew all about that. It wasn't the first time. But if I knew what was good for me, I'd keep quiet.'

The breakdown train from Wexford went north at 7.30 a.m. the next morning to find the engine on the sleepers but still upright and behind it the chasses of the burnt-out carriages. It was now a matter of routine to pull the engine and the wrecked coaches back on to the line and repair the railway. By 1 p.m. on19 January the main line was again open for traffic.

STAGED COLLISION AT PALACE EAST

Palace East/*Pailís Thoir* was a very sleepy little junction in mid-Wexford where the Dublin& South Eastern Railway (D&SER) line from Macmine Junction to Waterford met the Great Southern & Western Railway line that came from Dublin and Carlow through the Blackstairs Mountains. It was never a busy junction as the D&SER made no effort to make connections between its trains and those of a rival company providing an alternative route to Dublin. Palace East station stood on top of the watershed between the River Slaney to the east and the River Barrow to the west, with steeply falling gradients of 1 in 60 on either side of the station. The surrounding terrain may now look tame enough among the foothills of the Blackstairs Mountains, but during the Civil War years it was the focus of much anti-Treaty action directed at causing maximum damage to the railways.

Inspector Forde believed that these mountain borderlands had always been sanctuaries for outlaws and that their tradition dictated lack of respect for any authority or any government. He told Dr Hadden: 'These mountainy folk were an awful law-breaking crowd. Out for loot and what they could get out of the troubles. When they held up a train they took everything but the engine!' Inspector Forde was emphatic in his opinion that the root of the trouble on both sides of New Ross lay in local disloyalty among the company's own staff, just as he believed that New Ross owed its immunity to the personality of Dan O'Brien, its very popular little station master. However, unknown to Inspector Forde and the company, Palace House close to the station at Palace East was actually the centre of operations during the whole insurgent campaign and was a meeting place for the Brigade Council of the anti-Treaty forces. It was the property of the late Alfred Lyne and Palace East station stood on a corner of the property, with a private avenue leading from it to Palace House. In 1922 the station master at Palace East was named Holden, whose brother was active in the anti-Treaty forces. In later years Dr Peadar Sinnott told Dr George Hadden: 'It was extraordinary how

Palace East station, Co Wexford in 1960, looking towards New Ross.

the place escaped suspicion during those very active months. But towards the
end of February 1923, it was unmasked and occupied by the military. Alfred
Lyne was actually in the house at the time, but the womenfolk smuggled him
out to a lorry in a sack amongst the bedding and other household equipment
they were permitted to remove.' Alfred Lyne spent the ensuing months on
White Mountain near Polmounty Pass.

On 20 January 1923, immediately after the ambush at Scarawalsh when
the Civil War was reaching the peak of exasperation that ushered in its final
collapse, anti-Treaty forces attacked Palace East station shortly after 10 a.m.
They seized two trains in the station and destroyed two of the best engines
owned by the D&SER. At 10 a.m. the delayed 6.30 a.m. goods train from
Waterford to Wexford had arrived from the west hauled by 0-6-0 engine No
51. Shortly afterwards, the 9.45 a.m. passenger train from Macmine Junction
to Waterford arrived from the east hauled by 4-4-0 engine No 68, the very
same engine that had been recovered from the Scarawalsh ambush near
Enniscorthy just 36 hours earlier. Inspector Forde happened to be on the
footplate of No 68 that morning and was able to give a first-hand account of
what subsequently transpired.

But something went wrong. No 25 was still stopped on the bank when one of the captors, Peadar Sinnott, happened to glance idly behind him and 'the hair rose on my head. There rushing down on me through the darkness of a starless night and breathing smoke and flame like a dragon was No 56.' It was a terrifying apparition, driverless, insensate, dead, with open throttle and throwing off, as only a driverless engine can, vast clouds of expanding steam glowing red in the reflected glare from the engine and lit from within by a blazing volcano of sparks shot through the chimney from a tortured fire torn up by the fierce draught. Driver Hogan and Fireman Lee jumped off the footplate and Peadar Sinnott 'with an instinct to run, I leaped for the regulator and pulled it wide open. Then I jumped, bolting down the bank like a shot rabbit!' Immediately the descending demon hit No 25.

There was nobody to see what followed. No 25 had steam in its cylinders and was straining to be off. The rude thrust of No 56 through its crumbling tender was all that was needed to start No 25 moving. Off it went down the steep gradient, through the tunnel and across the long Barrow Bridge. Spraying the countryside with sparks, it raced through New Ross where it was seen by the startled Ganger Carton and Station Master O'Brien. At last, it ran to a stop some distance further on in a hollow near Glenmore station for lack of steam. Meanwhile No 56, using the wrecked tender as a ploughshare was tearing up the tracks under itself until finally it bogged

D&SER 4-4-0 engine No 56 after the bad collission at Ballyanne on the night of 10 January 1923.

down in the devastation it had created. The next morning Driver Hogan went to Glenmore to recover No 25 and found enough water in the boiler to work the 'Old Greyhound' back to New Ross station.

To the men who shared that episode on Ballyanne bank, it was the experience of a lifetime. Driver Hogan recalled:

> I got out of her with a few seconds to spare and it added ten years to my age. And in the dark we'd stopped within a few yards of one of the great embankment bridges, where we'd have jumped down a sheer 80 feet from the footplate on to the county road.

Dr Peadar Sinnott, who was one of the attackers on the footplate of No 25 that night, recalled:

> Just so, I've been in some tight corners, but that was the worst. The crash came as I was going down the bank. And I remember when I was picking myself up out of the fence at the bottom, hearing something heavy, a buffer perhaps, plunge into the field 100 yards away.

Some thirty years after the Civil War, Dr Hadden asked his medical colleague Dr Sinnott to make contact with his old lieutenant to try and find out what caused No 56 to appear so suddenly in full flight at Ballyanne bank that night. He found that, due either to the fired imagination or the over-excited nerves of the attackers at Rathgarogue, they were certain they had heard an earlier whistle 'coming down the wind from New Ross'. Therefore, No 56 had appeared even before No 25 had begun to run back to meet it for the staged collision. Indeed, it is interesting and quite characteristic of the people and the period, that Dr Peadar Sinnott had been from time to time attending professionally at Driver Michael Hogan's house for years afterwards and that neither had known, until Dr Hadden began his investigations, that they shared together an experience that neither of them would ever forget!

The morning after the crash on Ballyanne bank, the breakdown train's first problem was how to get through from Wexford to the scene of the destruction. The 26 wagons of pigs were still at the platform at Rathgarogue, where there was neither a passing loop nor a siding. There was also a three-mile haul mostly uphill back to Palace East, which no available engine could handle. Eventually two engines were found to haul the pigs out of the way and allow the breakdown train to get through. The repair gang found that a section of the railway had been ploughed up for over 100 yards, but with screw-presses they straightened out the rails and relaid them. It was now a matter of routine to get No 56 and the coaches back on the rails, but the tender of No 25 had to be abandoned as scrap.

In compensation, the government gave the D&SER a brand new tender, but according to Sketch White: 'It was far too good for the poor "Old Greyhound" whose best days were behind her'. The new tender was in fact given to a new engine. By 4.30 p.m. on 11 January 1923, Inspector Forde's breakdown gang had restored the railway on Ballyanne bank and the 26 wagons of pigs were finally sent through to Waterford only one day late.

STEAMING ON THE COUNTY ROAD

Within a week of the staged crash on Ballyanne bank the attackers returned to Rathgarogue on 16 January 1923 to hold up the same train, the afternoon mixed from Macmine Junction to Waterford. On that evening, unbelievably, it was hauled by No 17, the very same engine that featured in the 1900 Harcourt Street accident and also in the Bridge 399 accident at Killurin in July 1922. Behind the 0-6-0 engine was one six-wheel coach and 10 wagons of cattle. The cattle wagons were unhooked at the platform at Rathgarogue and the engine and coach were taken on to the Ballyanne bank. Here the attackers had broken the railway over the Old Ballyanne Bridge and pulled it to the edge of the 75 feet escarpment. There they sent the engine over with its coach. Immediately No 17 capsized, but in some extraordinary fashion it lay where it fell.

D&SER engine No 17 with one six-wheel coach sent over Ballyanne bank by anti-Treaty forces on 16 January 1923.

Inspector Forde described No 17 as 'overhanging the bank and looking from below as if she'd crash down at any moment'. But still the engine refused to move. When the breakdown gang arrived the coach was standing by the rails and could be sent back to Rathgarogue to join the cattle wagons already there. The engine, however, was lying head down at an angle of 45 degrees just below the edge of the bank with its tender still fouling the rails. No 17 certainly presented some problems. For instance, how to apply lifting jacks to an engine on such a slope? In the precarious position in which it was poised, there was no knowing what would happen once the engine was even slightly moved. What was quite certain, however, was that if any power did put the engine on its wheels where it lay, No 17 would toboggan right down the bank and nothing could stop it. So Inspector Forde decided to leave the engine where it was for the time being and merely deflect the railway around the wreck by creating a pair of temporary reverse eight-chain curves, over which traffic could pass at a restricted speed of 15 mph.

When the breakdown gang eventually got round to dealing with No 17, they laid a slide of sleepers down the bank before it and then, with the aid of a Thompson's endless-chain block hooked to a tree beyond the county road below, they slewed the engine round and slid it down on its side head-first to the toe of the bank. There they jacked the engine on to its wheels and laid rails under it. Then they raised steam and ran No 17 on the county road, just as it had previously run along city streets in Dublin after the Harcourt Street accident on St Valentine's Day 1900. The breakdown gang had only six pairs of light 24-feet flange rails, less than 48 yards in all. They used no sleepers but laid the rails independently on the road surface, gauge-held by tie-bars.

Once it was steamed the engine never stopped, but it crawled at snail-pace. As it cleared one pair of rails, they were detached and rushed around ahead to be bolted in position ready for No 17 when it reached them. Every man in the gang had his own job. There were men to unlock the fishplates behind; men to carry round the rails to the front; and men to lay the tie-rods and direct the alignment. As Dr Hadden was told: 'A skilled job and a busy job, even a tageous job!' There were a lot of rail lengths needed in running a mile of road. In fact, there were 220 lengths, but once they got moving it was not a particularly long job. So, with run and carry, No 17 was slowly worked under its own steam along the county road rising 76 feet in one mile. At Ballintubber cutting at the head of the rise where the road came level with the railway, they cut in on the line and ran the engine back on to the railway.

And so they brought No 17 back to Wexford under its own steam. 'A powerful strength those engines have,' said Michael Forde, 'except when they meet anything hard like themselves. Just get them back on the rails and work them away!' No truer words could be spoken of No 17, the miraculous

The 'tageous' job of running temporary track ahead of steaming engine No 17 along the county road after its derailment on the Ballyanne bank.

Bemused locals watch engine No 17 steaming along the public road below Ballyanne bank, on top of which engine No 68 awaits its slow return to the railway.

engine that survived crashing through the outer wall of Harcourt Street terminus Dublin in 1900, jumping across wrecked Bridge 399 at Killurin in July 1922 and, finally, falling down Ballyanne bank in January 1923.

DAN DOYLE'S REVENGE

According to Sketch White, drivers occasionally blew part of the fire out of their steam engines in order to clean out the tubes. 'Usually,' he said, 'they do it in a tunnel where they can't be seen and where they won't set the neighbourhood on fire. There was once,' he continued, 'a station master at New Ross/ *Ros Mhic Treoin* named Murphy – a crotchety man and unpopular. He had the mowing of the grass along the permanent way and in summer his hay cocks were clustered by the line.'

'One day, for some long-forgotten reason, he got Dan Doyle properly annoyed, Dan being then a happy and devil-may-care driver. As Dan was taking his engine out of the station, the sight of Murphy's haycocks flashed an idea into his mind. The wind was right and, as he ran past them, he turned on a full blast of steam through his engine and showered those cocks with half the contents of his firebox. And he went his way, leaving an exasperated, angry and completely helpless man to superintend the conflagration!'

New Ross station with a train about to depart for Macmine Junction headed by 0-6-0 engine No 354.

TROUBLE ON THE TUAM LINE

The market town of Tuam/ *Tuaim* in Co Galway was particularly hard hit by railway disruptions during the Civil War period. Destruction and derailments on the line connecting the town with the Dublin-Galway main line some 16 miles to the south at Athenry became so frequent that services were brought to a standstill on 10 July 1922 for five consecutive days. The Great Southern & Western Railway (GS&WR) responsible for the Limerick-Sligo line that served Tuam were very slow to carry out repairs that most probably would be nullified in a very short time. But their realistic attitude gave rise to an outburst of anger in Tuam and, eventually, even in Dáil Éireann.

An irate writer complained bitterly to the *Tuam Herald*:

I read two weeks ago where an announcement by the GS&WR stated that a full resumption of its train services had taken place. So little interest do they take in the section leading to Tuam or the people it is supposed to serve, I am of the opinion they do not recognise us – shades of Cromwell! If trains have been put on, we here in Tuam have not seen them.

The GS&WR since it took over from the Waterford & Limerick Railway has never properly served this district as it might have done. Consequently our fairs and businesses are suffering. The Local District Council and Tuam Commissioners should take up this matter on behalf of the people and if the GS&WR cannot improve matters, it should be called on to hand over the line to someone or some company who knows how to run it in the interests of and for the convenience of the public.

But on 20 July 1922 Crumlin Bridge near Ballyglunin station some six miles south of Tuam was blown up causing further delay in restoring rail services. When a partial service was restored three small bridges, as well as Crumlin Bridge for a second time, were completely destroyed by anti-Treaty forces on 23 September and the track was extensively damaged.

The GS&WR's reluctance to effect repairs quickly enough was condemned by the Tuam Commissioners and the town's traders, who called on the new Irish Free State government to have the repairs carried out and services restored. The absence of rail services was causing not only serious damage to local businesses and cattle fairs, but was also responsible for the laying-off of up to 50 railway employees in the area. On 29 September the metal bridge over the Ballinderry river south of Ballyglunin was blown up just after a goods train from Limerick had passed over it – so closely that the guard reported his van was shaken violently by the blast. In fairness to the GS&WR, great efforts were made by their engineering staff to repair the damaged bridges, but they were continually hampered by intimidation from anti-Treaty sympathisers and on three occasions during September they were fired on.

When attention was drawn in Dáil Éireann on 5 October 1922 to the great hardship being suffered by the people of Tuam and surrounding districts due to the enforced suspension of railway services, the government replied that delays in effecting repairs were due to the continued attacks on the line and not to any lack of repair funds, but that it was 'hoped to have the repairs carried out soon'. By mid-October 1922 every bridge along the entire 16 miles section between Tuam and Athenry had been blown up and even those previously repaired had again been destroyed. On 4 November 1922 the signal cabin at Ballyglunin was burned down, prompting the frustrated GS&WR to lodge a compensation claim of £2,100 with the government.

The continual acts of sabotage on the Athenry–Tuam section of the Limerick-Sligo line were caused mainly by anti-Treaty forces operating in and around Ballyglunin, the intermediate station some six miles south of Tuam. During the Civil War period Ballyglunin was the scene of several outrageous incidents. On 18 November 1922 an attempt was made by anti-Treaty forces to send a driverless train at full speed into Tuam, but fortunately government troops arrived just in time to prevent this outrage. Then on 8 December and again on 14 December the Limerick-Sligo goods train was raided at Ballyglunin and many items on board were stolen, including two barrels of Guinness, 56 pounds of butter, 5,000 cigarettes, four bags of flour, two sides of bacon and no less than 48 Christmas cakes. Clearly the raiders were stocking-up for their Christmas party! On several further occasions before Christmas the goods store in Ballyglunin station was raided, principally for spirits and bacon. Finally, on Christmas Eve 1922, the Limerick-Tuam evening passenger train was held-up by armed anti-Treaty forces at Ballyglunin station and the identities of passengers were examined. Following these serious incidents, the government ordered that Ballyglunin station be protected on a 24-hour basis by an army guard.

Probably because of this latter development, the anti-Treaty forces changed tactics in the New Year and held up trains well outside the station. The most serious incident occurred on 6 January 1923 when anti-Treaty forces held up the Limerick-Sligo goods train about one mile north of Ballyglunin by waving a red lamp. The train crew were then ordered at gunpoint to descend to the ground while the raiders removed a very large consignment of whiskey and bacon from a wagon of sundry goods destined for Tuam. Tim Bray, the goods train driver, was ordered to uncouple the 0-6-0 engine No 182 from the train, set it in motion and then jump off. Meanwhile, the train guard was compelled to release the brake in his van causing all the wagons to roll down a steep gradient back into Ballyglunin station. The army guard stationed there reacted quickly, but by the time reinforcements reached the scene of the hold-up the raiders had scattered taking with them their ill-gotten gains, but not before they had dispatched the driverless train engine on its way to Tuam. Shortly afterwards No 182 hurtled through Tuam station, demolishing the station level crossing gates as well as those on the Galway Road before coming to a stop near the site of the Sugar Factory, later built on the northern outskirts of the town. Most fortunately nobody was injured. The runaway locomotive had come to grief because a rail had been maliciously dislodged there to cause a crash of the following morning's Sligo-Limerick passenger train.

This most serious incident of 6 January 1923 so outraged the authorities that it was decided to introduce a special armoured train, named *King Tutankhamen*, to patrol the Athenry-Tuam section of the Limerick-Sligo line and to arrest the perpetrators so as to prevent further disruptions to rail services. As a result of this development, four local men were subsequently captured and controversially sent to Limerick Gaol. There they were later executed in one of the shameful revenge killings of that period. When the Civil War came to an end in April 1923, the GS&WR lodged with the government a claim for compensation in respect of the damage caused to the Athenry-Tuam section during the 1922-23 strife. The total claim amounted to the enormous sum, by 1923 standards, of £96,000.

Rail traffic slowly returned to normal after the end of the Civil War in Co Galway. On 7 October 1923 some 400 passengers travelled from Tuam to Dublin for a football match at a return fare of seven shillings and six pence. Following the monthly fair shortly afterwards, 3,000 pigs were loaded at Tuam station, as well as 5,742 cattle and sheep. The November Fair produced even greater volumes of rail traffic with 2,742 cattle, 4,623 sheep and 44 goats being dispatched in special trains from the station. The *Tuam Herald* was full of praise for the local railway staff:

> Great praise is due for the work done by all sections of the local rail staff. They provided a service in very difficult circumstances to the benefit of the town and surrounding area, ending their starvation and isolation.

The formidable armoured train, *King Tutankhamen*, in 1922/23.

In celebration of normality being restored, the Tuam Railway Social Club held a very successful dance in the local Wool Store on Saturday 19 April 1924. Admission cost twelve shillings for gentlemen; eight shillings for ladies; or a double-ticket could be bought for seventeen shillings and six pence. A large crowd of over 600 attended.

INTO THE SEA AT SLIGO

By the end of December 1922, any hopes of success by the anti-Treaty forces with a conventional military campaign had evaporated and their tactics changed to those of guerilla warfare, with the destruction of the railways as a high priority. Early in January 1923 the Sligo railway terminus of the Midland & Great Western Railway (M&GWR) was selected for destruction.

Shortly after midnight on 10 January a party of forty armed men from the First Battalion of the Third Western Division of the anti-Treaty forces descended on the large station at Sligo/*Sligeach* and systematically set about the work of destruction in a very thorough manner. The station master, Mr Hogg, and his family were aroused in their residence and ordered to dress at once, leave the premises and seek safety elsewhere. Petrol and explosives were then used to destroy the station and all that it contained. Two passenger trains within the terminus were completely burned out. In all, eighteen vehicles of rolling stock belonging to the M&GWR were totally destroyed.

The *Fermanagh Times* of 18 January reported:

Petrol and mines were used in the destruction of the station and the explosions shook the town. The building, which was one of the most solidly constructed of its kind in Ireland, is now a mass of debris.

The official report issued by the M&GWR in Dublin stated that armed men took possession of its station at Sligo and destroyed by fire the entire rolling stock and station premises. The report continued:

The rolling stock, which included passenger coaches, goods wagons, cattle trucks, horse boxes, etc. were placed in line, sprinkled with petrol and then set on fire. The station buildings were similarly treated and were completely burned. The raiders remained until they assured themselves that the work of destruction was well advanced and on leaving warned the railway employees not to attempt to extinguish the flames.

The Railway Company, notwithstanding its heavy loss, are running trains to and from Sligo as usual.

Original Sligo railway station which was totally burned down by anti-Treaty forces on 10 January 1923.

The steeply-sloping branch line from Sligo station down which seven engines were sent into the sea.

Significantly, the official report made no reference whatever to the other most embarrassing feature of the raid on Sligo station – the fact that all the engines in the terminus that night were assembled, coupled together and then sent down the steeply inclined branch to the sea at the deep-water berths on Sligo Quay!

The story of that most audacious and destructive venture in the history of Irish railways is fascinating. While the station terminus was being burned, another party of armed men boldly entered the locomotive shed where seven engines were housed – five belonging to the M&GWR and two the property of the Sligo Leitrim & Northern Counties Railway (SL&NCR) that operated services for passengers and goods between Sligo and Enniskillen. The engine cleaning staff was held at gunpoint and preparations were made to move all the engines out on to the main line. Three of the engines were in steam and these were used to pull out the line of seven engines to Magheraboy Bridge, a short distance out from Sligo. Then the points just outside Sligo station leading from the main line into the one mile branch down the 1 in 70 incline to Sligo Quay were set to receive a train.

The *Sligo Champion* of 13 January described what happened:

When the engines were got on to the main line, they were coupled together and with the aid of the locomotives under steam, were drawn out as far as Magheraboy Bridge. The points appear to have been set so that an incoming train would be switched on the line leading to the goods store and the deep-water berths. When the engines were started, they dashed along at a tremendous pace aided by the incline. The heavy string of engines gathered terrible speed and smashed through the stop buffer as if it were only a small heap of sand and through the solid concrete breakwater. One of the engines fell completely into the sea, another a large new express locomotive No 104 hung across the wall, while the remaining ones were hurled into all sorts of positions.

Between the M&GWR and the SL&NCR, over twenty carriages were completely burned in the station, only the steel framework remaining. Over ten wagons were set on fire and four of these were destroyed. In the words of the *Sligo Champion*: 'The station premises present a scene of ruin and desolation that beggars belief.' To crown the destruction achieved by the anti-Treaty forces, all seven engines in Sligo that night were consigned to their destruction in the deep-water berths at Sligo Quay. The total damage caused by the night's havoc was estimated to have been of the order of £100,000, a considerable sum in 1923.

Yet the railway companies showed their resilience. While they did not immediately restore services as implied in the official report released in

Various scenes showing the destruction of Sligo station and rolling stock by anti-Treaty forces.

Dublin, incoming trains on the following morning 11 January were able to bring their passengers to a point just outside the wrecked station and departures from Sligo resumed later that afternoon. But there was some considerable criticism of the ease with which the attackers were able to wreak havoc with apparent impunity. The Free State army garrison in Sligo was heavily criticised for its lack of response to an attack on a major railway terminus until an hour after it had started. It transpired that there had been no military guard on the station that night. According to the *Fermanagh Times*:

> Simultaneously with the outbreak of fire, the military posts at the Courthouse and jail were sniped at, but the attackers were quickly driven off. Troops which were rushed to the station were also fired upon and heavy machine-gun and rifle fire lasted a couple of hours. So far as is known, there were no casualties.

In Dáil Éireann it was admitted that 'the incident at Sligo had very serious aspects'. On 12 January 1923 an editorial in *The Irish Times* concluded: 'If the garrison lacked neither vigilance nor efficiency, but was overpowered by superior numbers, the condition of the Sligo area is far worse than Eastern Ireland had been allowed to suppose.'

SMASH-UP AT STREAMSTOWN

Early in 1923 there was considerable destruction caused by anti-Treaty forces on the railways in Co Westmeath, especially on the then main Dublin-Galway line of the Midland & Great Western Railway (M&GWR) near Streamstown/*Baile an tSrutháin* station. This was a junction station between Mullingar and Athlone where a branch line diverged southwards to Clara in Co Offaly to join with the Great Southern & Western Railway line from Portarlington to Athlone. In all, no less than six engines of the M&GWR, together with much rolling stock, were badly damaged or destroyed in three separate incidents involving both main line and branch line trains, between 13 January and 17 February 1923.

The Railroad Protection and Maintenance Corps formed by the government the previous October proved quite ineffectual in preventing the

Streamstown junction station, Co Westmeath.

Wreckage of the Galway mail train at Steamstown, February 1923.

series of incidents near Streamstown. At the army inquiry in 1924 Charles Russell, who had been in charge of the Corps, complained that his units had enormous problems with quartermastering, which greatly limited their effectiveess. Referring to the incidents with anti-Treaty forces between Mullingar and Athlone, he told the inquiry: 'I prepared troops to try and outwit them. I had the troops standing to in the Griffith Barracks and they were just short of caps and leggings and rifles.' As a result, his men could not set out. It is interesting that Charles Russell testified that such problems persisted to the end of the Civil War. He was especially critical of the quality of the men provided for his Corps: 'All the commands threw all their "dud" officers, as they called them, into the Railway Corps – every one of them.'

With freedom to attack trains with impunity, the anti-Treaty forces indulged in spectacular wrecking at Streamstown. On 13 January a goods train from Dublin consisting of two engines and twenty-five wagons was stopped by armed men at the junction for Clara, the crew were removed and the train sent off at full speed to a break in the rails where the engines were derailed and wagons piled up on top. During the clearing-up operations, the permanent way gang was told not to be too particular, as the railroad would soon be broken again. In fact, within a few days, the engine of the Clara branch train was derailed at the very same spot.

However, the most spectacular incident in Co Westmeath occurred on 17

February 1923 when the Limited Mail from Dublin to Galway hauled by 4-4-0 engine No 124 was deliberately wrecked at about 9 a.m., together with two goods trains, close to Streamstown station. As the *Westmeath Guardian* reported on 23 February: 'The point near Streamstown where the outrage was committed is that at which not long since two other trains were wrecked.' It was about 300 yards west of Streamstown station where a bridge over the county road supported the railway. This bridge was damaged twice before, but had been repaired. However, during the night of 16 February it was blown up. The *Westmeath Guardian* graphically described what happened:

> It is understood armed men seized Streamstown signal cabin and placed the signals against the mail train. When it stopped, the passengers were ordered out. The train was then set towards the wrecked bridge, where it was completely destroyed. The crash of the wreckage was heard for miles around.
>
> The carriages were telescoped, among them being corridor and dining cars. The mail vans turned completely over. The great engine dashed over the embankment and now lies hanging above a field, whilst some of the carriages are also overhanging the lower ground and some are wrecked on the line.

Unbelievably, a further outrage was soon to follow. A long goods train coming from Ballina approached Streamstown from the west soon afterwards and was similarly held up by the armed men. It was also sent into the wrecked bridge at speed causing further wreckage and debris that 'piled up in a heap' according to local observers. Not yet being satisfied with the havoc

Wreckage of the triple train crash at Streamstown on 17 February 1923. This was the last serious Civil War incident on the M&GWR.

they had caused, the anti-Treaty attackers then stopped a train of empty goods wagons coming from Mullingar and heading west to Claremorris. This third train was then sent into the smashed and telescoped carriages and wagons already littering the countryside. As one passenger from the Limited Mail told the *Westmeath Guardian* reporter:

> I'll tell it briefly. There are three trains with carriages piled up as high as a big house, engines wrecked, Limited Mail engine in a field – a fearful scene of havoc and wreck.

A breakdown gang from Athlone arrived at the scene in mid-morning and had a new temporary bridge in place by that afternoon, allowing passengers to resume their journeys. Thankfully, no loss of life or limb was reported from any of the wrecking incidents at Streamstown. The big spectacular smash-up on 17 February 1923 proved to be the last serious incident involving the M&GWR in the Civil War period.

SABOTAGE IN KILKENNY

During the period of intense destructive action against the railways in the Civil War, two significant incidents took place in Co Kilkenny. A short passenger train from Maryborough (now Portlaoise) was totally derailed on the northern approach to Kilkenny/*Cill Chainnigh* and in the south of the county either a derailment or a massive explosion near Ballyhale/*Baile hÉile* caused an engine to topple down an embankment almost into the haggard of a lineside farm.

Compared with the counties of Munster or even with Wexford, Kilkenny suffered far less damage to its railways in the Civil War possibly because of its position outside the region intended by the anti-Treaty forces to be a 'Munster Republic'. When the new government's army began to enforce its authority in Dublin with the attack on the Four Courts on 28 June 1922, it quickly forced the surrender of the defiant anti-Treaty garrison lodged there on 5 July 1922 and moved on to secure control of the capital city and the province of Leinster, including Co Kilkenny. The anti-Treaty forces fell back on their strongholds in Connacht and Munster, ambitiously planning to establish their 'Munster Republic' south of the 'Limerick-Waterford Line' in order to frustrate the creation of an Irish Free State. But the government troops steadily advanced south and progressively won control over Limerick and Waterford in a conventional military fashion. By the use of naval landings on the Cork coast, they advanced on the city of Cork and captured it on 10 August 1922. Within days, the anti-Treaty forces had abandoned their conventional military strategies and had reverted to guerilla warfare. This caused the Civil War to drag on for a further eight months into the spring of 1923 and resulted in the widespread destruction of the railways.

While most of this destruction occurred in Counties Cork, Tipperary, Sligo, Galway and Wexford, Kilkenny did not escape unscathed. For example, statistics prepared by the Great Southern & Western Railway for a compensation claim lodged with the government for malicious damage caused by civil strife from 28 June to 31 December 1922 reveal surprising

Engine No 79 at the foot of the embankment at Ballyhale, Co Kilkenny on 29 December 1922. Note the hay ricks in the nearby haggard.

damage. In Co Kilkenny alone the railways suffered damage to permanent way at 18 locations, to bridges at ten locations, to signal cabins at six locations and to engines or rolling stock at four locations. Many of the more desperate attacks took place after the Irish Free State was officially established on 6 December 1922, when the full fury of the anti-Treaty guerillas was unleashed against the railways. It was during this latter period that the significant incidents referred to earlier took place.

Unfortunately, it is not possible to describe what exactly happened in these outrages. At the end of December 1922 the government imposed a complete news censorship on the local press in Co Kilkenny and as this remained in force until 24 February 1923, there is no news record of local happenings during that period of high destruction. No doubt the imposed news blackout facilitated the government in dealing ruthlessly with those guerillas causing the continual sabotage of the railways. Without local documentary evidence it is only possible to search national newspapers and scrutinise surviving photographs to try and guess what most likely happened at Ballyhale and Kilkenny at that time.

Railroad Protection & Maintenance Corps team at the scene of sabotage in south Kilkenny on 10 March 1923.

The 0-4-4T engine No 79 lying at the foot of an embankment near Ballyhale some 15 miles south of Kilkenny was photographed on 29 December 1922. It appears to have been either deliberately derailed or blown completely off the embankment by a powerful explosion that caused it to tumble down almost into the old-fashioned haggard shown in the photograph. The picture of the passenger train lying on its side was taken some four miles north of Kilkenny on 8 January 1923 at the former junction with the ten mile branch line built by the British government in 1919-1920 to facilitate the exploitation of coal deposits at Deerpark Colliery near Castlecomer. The 4-4-0 engine No 61 heading the passenger train of three six-wheeled carriages was the 7.30 p.m. Dublin-Kilkenny train coming from Maryborough which was then the junction on the Dublin-Cork main line serving Kilkenny and Waterford. A short reference to the incident appeared in *The Irish Times* of 10 January 1923:

The train was stopped by armed men who, having ordered the passengers to alight, caused the train to be again set in motion. A short distance further on some lengths of rail had been removed from the line and the train became derailed. The passengers, numbering about 50, were obliged to continue their journey to Kilkenny on foot. It is stated that, despite threats of being shot, the engine driver refused to restart the train.

While it appears that no casualties resulted from these particular acts of sabotage, it is certain that the trauma suffered by those unfortunate enough to have been involved in them, as in hundreds of other outrages committed during the shameful Civil War, caused great hurt and bitterness that has persisted down through the generations even into the twenty-first century.

Engine No 61 with its train totally derailed near Castlecomer junction, Kilkenny on 8 January 1923.

THE GREAT FLOUR ROBBERY

When the new Irish Free State began to exert its authority by securing control over dissident towns towards the end of 1922, the occupation of Tralee in Co Kerry by government troops obliged anti-Treaty forces to entrench themselves westward throughout the Dingle Peninsula. Many railway and road bridges had been blown up in this area and west of Tralee all railway traffic on the Tralee & Dingle Railway was disrupted. For several months no trains had run on this narrow-gauge line or on its branch line from Lower Camp (officially Castlegregory Junction) to Castlegregory. With the onset of winter, the threat of food shortage loomed and actual hunger was very real.

The Fourth Battalion of the Kerry Brigade of anti-Treaty forces based in Camp learned that a food ship had left Cork for Dingle and Ballykissane Pier, near Killorglin on the Iveragh Peninsula, and that it was laden with a large consignment of St Louis flour and other goods. Much of the flour was intended for Killarney Mental Hospital that, in those turbulent times, could only be supplied by sea through Ballykissane Pier. The vessel duly arrived off Dingle/*An Daingean*, hove to and cast anchor awaiting high tide. An elaborate plan had been devised by the Kerry Brigade to gain possession of that valuable consignment of flour. The ship would be hijacked and forced into Dingle harbour at night, where a multitude of horses-and-carts would be organised to convey the plundered flour from the quayside to the railway. There it would be loaded into wagons of a specially commandeered train that would distribute the badly needed flour to households known to be 'friendly to the cause'.

The story of the celebrated 'Midnight Flour Special' was recorded by Walter McGrath of Cork from the surviving fireman of that train, Paddy Martin a native of Dingle/*An Daingean*:

> I was then a fireman, and later a driver, of the Dingle Railway. No trains had run for months and one night I was sitting in my home in John Street, Dingle, when two armed volunteers entered and ordered me to

get up to the station immediately and get steam up in an engine, as a food train was to be run to Camp. I demurred at first, but a gun was quickly produced!

I was then told a party of officials had earlier hijacked a ship in Dingle harbour and had brought it to the pier, where a large number of carts were lined up. Tons upon tons of flour and some other goods were unloaded from the ship on to the carts and driven up to the railway station.

When Paddy Martin got to the station he found one engine already in steam. It had come all the way from Castlegregory, under Driver Tom Bailey and Fireman Jerry O'Donovan, also under 'armed guard'. Driver Jack Cotter and Paddy, as fireman, then set about getting a fire going in the Dingle engine's firebox, while all the time wagon after wagon was being loaded up with the bags of flour from the horse-carts. Paddy continued:

Eventually we set off double-headed for Camp. There was supposed to be an armed lorry following us on the road, which ran near the track for long stretches. There were also armed men on the train.

My only memory of the strange journey is that at Annascaul, Station Master Bob Knightly was waiting for us. On re-starting, he travelled with us for a short distance and pointed out some 'friendly' houses where we threw out a few sacks of flour to waiting hands.

The train continued through the dark night up the long climb through Emalough and Glenmore to the summit of Glenagalt/*Gleann na nGealt*. Ghostly it must then have seemed winding its way down the steep incline into Camp and across Camp Viaduct to reach Castlegregory Junction at Lower Camp. There the greatest scenes of activity were witnessed. Tom Francis was only a child, but he remembers the mysterious hustle and bustle and the night-long comings and goings of carts and traps. Tom's father had been station master at Castlegregory Junction/*Gabhal Chaisleáin Ghriaire*, but had died two years earlier.

Joe Spillane, one of the best-known residents of Fermoyle on the road to Cloughane not far from the Connor Pass, was a young volunteer in the anti-Treaty forces billeted in Camp during the early months of the Civil War. He remembered well that night:

I travelled on the famous 'flour train' in both directions. I went west to Dingle with the Castlegregory engine, as one of the unit in action, and returned to the Junction after the sacks of flour had been loaded. It was a mysterious journey. [Joe's wife, Mrs Bridget Spillane, interjected at this point with her memories.]

Double-headed Tralee & Dingle line train similar to that used in the Great Flour Robbery.

I often heard that the whole countryside was saturated with St Louis flour for weeks after the incident. There was more than flour. There was tea in timber chests – and I can tell you there were many cans of sweets going the rounds too!

Pat O'Shea of Castlegregory had the last word for Walter McGrath. He would not comment on whether the whole affair had been an important military exercise or not. He presumed some of the flour in the Camp area, and around Killelton and Derrymore, had probably been put to good use. Before long, however, the Free State troops arrived in Castlegregory and the hidden stocks of flour were soon unearthed. 'Alas,' said Pat, 'for the clever plans of mice and men in times of Civil War!'

TOPPLED INTO THE ABYSS

The Waterford Dungarvan & Lismore Railway was the most difficult route of any of the five railways that radiated from Waterford city. It was also one of the most scenic lines in the south of Ireland winding its way first along the banks of the River Suir, then capturing breathtaking views of the Comeragh Mountains on its right before descending steeply at 1 in 66 beyond Kilmacthomas and Durrow to capture spectacular views on its left of the sea at Clonea and the magnificent bay of Dungarvan. To capture such vistas major engineering works were required, including a brick-faced tunnel at Durrow and massive stone viaducts at Kilmacthomas, Durrow and Ballyvoile/ *Baile an Phoill*. It was at the latter viaduct over a deep ravine in January 1923 that one of the most spectacular railway incidents of the Civil War period occurred. An engineering works train was commandeered and sent towards the high Ballyvoile Viaduct that had already been blown up

A view of Ballyvoile Viaduct, Co Waterford, prior to its destruction by anti-Treaty forces in August 1922. Note the road bridge in the foreground.

no wagons to detach or pick-up at Ardfert station and was not checked by any red light, the engine began to gather speed for the final leg of its journey to Tralee. When it hit the broken section of the line, the engine was derailed and sent plunging down the steep embankment on the right-hand side of the line, carrying with it 17 laden wagons.

The guard in the brake van at the rear of the train felt the shock and applied his brake, resulting in his van and 9 wagons remaining on the track. Although badly knocked about and severely bruised, he left his van and went up to the front of the train to find only wrecked wagons in the field below and the engine lying on its side. He called the driver and fireman by their names but got no response. Then in almost total darkness Guard John Galvin crept down the steep embankment and near the engine he found Fireman Daniel Crowley of Cork lying on the ground very badly scalded. 'Don't mind me, save Paddy,' the poor fireman kept on repeating as steam and boiling water were pouring from the locomotive. The guard pulled the fireman away from the wreckage and made him as comfortable as possible on the grass.

With the aid of his paraffin handlamp, Guard Galvin began to search for the driver, Patrick O'Riordan of Tralee. He found him buried beneath the engine hood with his legs stretched out from the footplate. He tried to extricate him but his efforts were in vain and he feared that Paddy was already dead. John Galvin then set off to seek help from the milesman's house. There he found the shocked milesman just released from captivity by the raiders who had vanished into the darkness as soon as the train had crashed down the embankment. Both men carried the severely scalded fireman to a house nearby and sought help from Tralee. A detachment of the army soon arrived from Tralee with an ambulace, but had great difficulty in releasing Driver O'Riordan from beneath the engine. As feared he was pronounced dead on arrival at Tralee Infirmary. Fireman Crowley was still conscious when he arrived there but he only lingered until about 2.00 a.m. the following morning when he died from severe scalding.

A subsequent inquest heard that the driver died from multiple and horrific injuries and the fireman from severe burning of the face and hands due to scalding. The coroner praised the efforts of both the guard and milesman in trying to alleviate the horrible sufferings of the engine crew. The funeral of Driver Patrick O'Riordan was one of the largest gatherings ever seen in Tralee, while the internment of Fireman Daniel Crowley drew a huge outpouring of sympathy in Cork.

General public outrage following the Ardfert incident had a very negative effect on the tacit support hitherto given to the anti-Treaty forces in Kerry. Over the following months public enthusiasm slowly began to wane for those who were resisting the authority of the new government of the Irish Free

An armoured Lancia car adapted for railway use during the Civil War.

State. Within three months of the railway outrage at Ardfert, Comdt Frank Aiken as Chief of Staff of the anti-Treaty forces ordered a ceasefire and a dumping of arms on 24 April 1923, effectively ending the Irish Civil War.

PART THREE

TWENTIETH-CENTURY ACCIDENTS

THE OWENCARRROW VIADUCT DISASTER

County Donegal, at the north-western corner of Ireland, is sparsely populated. The land is mostly mountainous and poor and, until the late twentieth century, only its rugged coastline could provide even a meager subsistence for its small coastal farmers and fishermen. It was not surprising, therefore, that railway entrepreneurs of the nineteenth century tended to avoid the county. The vast expanse of West Donegal failed to attract any railways until the early 1890s. The Light Railways (Ireland) Act 1889 enabled state aid to be provided in the form of a free grant towards the cost of construction of light railways and this enabled narrow-gauge lines to be opened as far as Killybegs and Glenties. But the poorest regions in the far north-west were left without railways until The Light Railways Act 1896 enabled substantial state aid to be made available to stimulate development in areas designated as 'congested districts', which included much of north-west Co Donegal. It was under this Act that the Letterkenny & Burtoport Extension Railway was built over a distance of 80 kilometres mainly to serve the herring fishing industry. Opened in1903, it effectively extended the main line of the Londonderry & Lough Swilly Railway (L&LSR) beyond Letterkenny through the finest and wildest scenery to be found on any Irish railway. However, it included bleak and treeless areas open to the full force of the Atlantic gales.

A few short years after the opening of the Burtonport Extension, two carriages of a train were lifted by a cross wind and derailed as it traversed the 350 metre-long Owencarrow Viaduct south of Creeslough/*An Chraoslach* on a very exposed section of the line. The vehicles were held on the viaduct by the iron railing and nobody was injured.

Almost twenty years later, on 7 February 1923, bad weather came in from the west and hurricane-force winds roared over the Rosses, the most westerly section of the line where there is scarcely a bush for shelter. The first train left Burtonport that morning at 8.30 a.m. with three passengers aboard.

A Burtonport-Derry mixed train seen crossing Owencarrow Viaduct early in the twentieth century.

On a very exposed section between Kincasslagh and Crolly the train was on a falling gradient on a three-metre embankment above the surrounding rock and bog, when a tremendous gust lifted three of the four vehicles and tipped them down the bank. Only the third brake van was left on the rails, separated from the engine by a gap of some thirty metres. The shaken passengers were assisted to shelter in the van, while the driver went ahead to Crolly to seek help. By the time he returned, another great gust had swept the line clear!

But by far the worst accident caused by the Atlantic gales in Ireland occurred on Friday 30 January 1925 while a train was crossing the Owencarrow Viaduct. It was the 5.15 p.m. from Derry to Burtonport, made up of the large 4-6-2 tank engine No 14, drawing a covered wagon, a six-wheeled carriage, a bogie carriage, and a combined carriage and van. The train had left Kilmacrennan at 7.52 p.m. and would have reached the viaduct about 8 p.m. The passengers on board that windy night had no idea of the impending tragedy. The evening train on a winter's night was frequently buffeted by high winds and regular passengers took little note of it. As Pádraig Ua Cnáimhsí described it sixty years later in *Glór Ghaoth Dobhair*:

> Ba mhinic an traen chéanna ar a cosán oíche gaoithe móire roimhe sin agus ní dhéarnadh a dhath ar bith uirthe. Bhíodh solas geas acu ins na carraistí an t-am sin agus bhíodh cuideachta bhreá ag pasantóirí uirthe — ag inse scéaltach, ag comhrá le chéile, ag ceol agus mar sin de. Ba annamh oíche nach mbíodh fear leat ar an traen a mbíodh leath-phionta leis as Leitir Ceanainn nó ó Dhoire, agus bhíodh sé ar obair ag ól súimín as go dtí go mbéadh deireadh ólta aige. Ligfeadh sé anuas an fhuinneog ansin agus chaithfeadh sé ar shiúl an buidéal a bhíodh folamh. Chuaigh an oíche thárt gasta go leor mar sin.

The carriages were lit by gaslight and there was always good company on board, with the time being passed telling stories, exchanging gossip and singing songs. There was seldom a night when someone in the company had not taken with them some extra bottles of stout from Letterkenny or even Derry for the long train journey home. Slowly these 'extras' would be consumed amid much chat and laughter, with occasional brief lowering of the window to cast out the empty bottles. In this happy mood did the passengers begin to cross the long and exposed Owencarrow Viaduct, impervious to the gale roaring down from Muckish Mountain towards the unfortunate train.

The train driver, Robert McGuinness from Derry, later described to the public inquiry what then transpired:

> After travelling about sixty yards (over the viaduct) I again looked back and, seeing the sidelights of the Guard's van, considered that everything

The unpretentious terminus of the L&LSR at Graving Dock, Derry.

was right. The wind was gusty and I was proceeding at the ordinary reduced speed and, at the moment when I found it necessary to reach over to the regulator in order to maintain this speed, I again cast another glance back. I then noticed that the six-wheeled carriage was off the line and raised in the air. I at once applied the full force of the brake and pulled up almost immediately. At that time the carriage struck the wagon between it and the engine also sideways to the parapet.

The fireman, John Hannigan from Letterkenny, told the inquiry:

The first thing I noticed was the first carriage seeming to rise from the rails. At that moment the driver, having also noticed something wrong, applied his brakes and brought the train to a standstill. I walked over to the other side and looked and said to the driver 'There is harm done tonight.' I got down first and he got down after me. He walked back to the van and got the guard out. When I was halfways over, there was a woman coming crawling up the bank; so I stopped and caught her hand and brought her to safety. Then there came three more up after that. They came up themselves.

The derailment happened above the embankment of granite boulders between the girder and the masonry parts of the viaduct. In the gloom the train crew could see that behind the six-wheeled carriage, the bogie carriage was clear of the track and lying on its side at the top of the slope, while the

Carriages of the ill-fated train blown off the Owencarrow Viaduct by a gale on 30 January 1925.

combined carriage was resting on the damaged bridge parapet. The six-wheeler was upside down and, wedged in mid-air between the first of the masonry arches and the bank, its leading end crushed in. The impact had brought away the complete roof and all within the carriage dropped to the rocks some sixteen metres below. The carriage brought with it some of the masonry of the viaduct and these heavy stones tumbled down on the injured passengers. Pádraig Ua Cnáimhsí described what happened:

> Am inteacht i ndiaidh an seacht a chlog, tháinig an traen anuas fríd An Bhéarnas agus rinne sí ar an droichead a bhí le na tabhairt trasna ar ghleann mhór a bhí roimpí. Ba le linn dí a bheith ag dul trasna an droichid a tharla an tubaiste. Shéid an gála gaoithe a bhí ann ceann de na carraistí ar shiúl ó na ráillí agus i ndiaidh de suí ansin cupla bomaite agus é ceaptha ag babhún an droichid ansin, thit an carraiste agus a raibh ann síos i lag a bhí ansin leithchéad troigh síos uaidh. Rinneadh smionagar de pháirt amháin den charraiste agus ba sa chuid sin a bhí na daoine a maríodh an oíche sin. As ádhmad a bhí na carraistí déanta an t-am sin agus ba léir nach raibh siad déanta láidir go leor mar sin chun titim den chineál sin a sheasamh. Le na chois sin go léir, is cosúil go dtug an carraiste leis cuid de na clocha a bhí i mbabhún an droichid agus gur thit na clocha sin síos sa mhullach ar an mhuintir a bhí gortaithe.

The train crew and passengers from the other carriages struggled in the gale and pitch darkness to rescue those trapped in the splintered remains of the six-wheeler, but it proved a most difficult task. Fortunately, a priest living nearby, Father Bearnaí Ó Gallchóir, reached the scene of the disaster and ministered to the injured and dying. In all, four passengers were killed and four more were seriously injured.

The four killed that night were all Gaelic-speaking people from north-west Donegal. They were Niall Ó Dúgáin from Mín Bun Abhann in the parish of Tearmann; Úna Ní Mholagáin from Fál Carrach; and a couple from the island of Árainn Mhór, Feidhlimí Ó Baoill and his wife Sorcha. Sitting with them in the same compartment was their young son, Feidhlimí Óg. He had a miraculous escape and lived his later adult life in Chicago until his death in 1984. Of the four who died in the tragedy, one survived that night and was brought to Letterkenny Hospital but sadly died the following morning, the eve of St Bridget's Day. The four victims were mourned by their neighbours, relatives and friends in wakes that were remembered as keenly as the tragedy of *Oíche an Droichid Mhóir* in the folk memory of west Donegal.

According to the Gaelic-speaking people of west Donegal, a public inquiry held subsequent to the Owencarrow Viaduct disaster yielded very little information that was not already known. It was stated during the inquiry that carriages used on this line should be constructed of steel, rather than timber that splintered in accidents of this kind. But this was not recommended in the inquiry's report. A decision was taken shortly afterwards, however, that all carriages used on the Burtonport Extension should be fitted with heavy iron plates as ballast to prevent any future incidents of trains being blown off the rails by Atlantic gales. The Londonderry & Lough Swilly Railway purchased 280 cast iron slabs, each weighing one hundredweight, for this purpose and one was placed in the corners of each compartment in the carriages designated for use on the Burtonport Extension. The government suggested that two anemometres should be erected to control traffic during storms. The company declined to have one on the viaduct, as this would have involved a semi-resident staff, but one was erected on an exposed site at Dunfanaghy Road station. The readings were regularly sent to the relevant government department and in January 1927 the anemometre justified its existence by recording a gust of no less than 112mph!

All that remains today of the Owencarrow Viaduct is a line of lonely masonry columns standing in a windswept glen to remind us, as the Donegal Gaelic storytellers do, of 'oíche an ghálaidh mhóir fadó an t-am a maraíodh agus a gortaíodh daoine ansin, am nach raibhtheas ag dréim le na leithéid maith nó olc.'

THE STEAMROLLER COLLISION

To open up the areas to the northwest of Cork city, a narrow-gauge railway system was authorised under the 1883 Tramways Act and built initially to Blarney, with later extensions to Coachford and Donaghmore which was reached in 1893. It was known as the Cork & Muskerry Light Railway and from its terminus at Western Road in Cork it served the largely agricultural region of East Muskerry from which it took its name. Until its closure in 1934, it carried tourists to Blarney Castle, commuters into and out of Cork, and the produce and livestock of the districts it served. Being a light railway cheaply constructed, long stretches of its track ran along a reservation at the side of the public road. This feature was responsible for one of the most curious accidents on an Irish railway.

On 6 September 1927 the morning train from Donaghmore was slowly proceeding along the side of the road near Carrigrohane/*Carrig Ruacháin*, when a steamroller working on the surfacing of the road crashed into the

The scene on 6 September 1927 after a steamroller crashed into the Donaghmore-Cork train at Carrigrohane on the Cork & Muskerry Light Railway.

Carrigrohane, Co Cork after the steamroller crashed into the Donaghmore-Cork train on 6 September 1927.

train damaging and derailing the two leading coaches. The train that morning was hauled by 4-4-0T engine No 8K and consisted of four carriages, six goods wagons and a brake van. Fortunately nobody was injured, although several lady passengers fainted. The cause of the accident was never explained.

The local wags, however, noting that the accident had happened on the Carrigrohane Straight then renowned for its motor racing, declared that the steamroller and the train were having a race!

THE CLOGHER VALLEY RAILWAY

The Clogher Valley lies in the centre of the nine counties of Ulster, a region of good farmland where the northern Blackwater River begins its journey towards Lough Neagh. It is almost entirely in South Tyrone and takes its name from the ancient settlement of Clogher/ *Clochar*, an early royal and ecclesiastical seat. The region had little industry beyond that connected with agriculture, but it did boast a famous narrow-gauge railway that traversed a distance of some sixty kilometres between Maguire's Bridge in Co Fermanagh and Tynan in Co Armagh. At these places, the broad-gauge lines of the Great Northern Railway linked the Clogher Valley Railway with Enniskillen and Belfast.

The Clogher Valley line began its life in 1887 as a tramway, but by 1894 it had changed to a light railway that ran alongside the public road for much of its way. To ensure better safety, its six 0-4-2T engines ran backwards to give drivers a better view from the cab of the road ahead. For roadside running the engines were fitted with a large headlamp and a cowcatcher. The line's rolling stock consisted of thirteen passenger carriages, six parcel and brake vans, and over a hundred assorted goods wagons. These ranged from horseboxes to butter wagons, but the majority were wagons for the movement of cattle to and from the fairs. The bulk of the freight, apart from cattle, was timber, coal, meal and farm produce. There were trains carrying the mail and supplies to shops, including barrels of Guinness, and the daily milk train providing an essential service for the farming community. Passenger coaches ranged from the luxurious first-class carriages with inlaid wooden panels and leather upholstery to third-class vehicles with their plain perforated wooden seating.

Trains on the Clogher Valley Railway did not travel too fast. For many years prior to its closure in 1941, its theme song was said to be that sung by the famous Irish tenor of the time John Mc Cormack 'I'll Walk Beside You Through This Vale of Tears'! Yet on busy days, like the Twelfth of July or the Clogher Valley Show, there were not sufficient coaches to meet the demand.

A postcard view of a Clogher Valley train travelling through Main Street, Fivemiletown, Co Tyrone.

On such occasions, some of the wagons had to be fitted up with benches to carry additional passengers. The special trains run for these occasions often needed two engines and, sometimes, a third one pushing to get the train over Tullyvar Hill. This ordeal gave rise to the story that the guard ordered first-class passengers to stay where they were, but that third-class passengers were told 'get out and push!'

The Clogher Valley Railway was not only a light railway that ran along the side of the public road, but when it entered the small towns it usually ran up the middle of the main street. One of the more famous was Fivemiletown, Co Tyrone, where trains had to contend with many obstacles, including pedestrians, horse carts and steamrollers. A most unusual regular obstacle was Maggie Coulter's goat. The engine fireman had to pelt it with live coals to clear the line on the approach to Fivemiletown. Judging from a surviving photograph of the goat, it is likely that Maggie encouraged the goat to block the line because his regular obstructing tactics ensured that she was seldom short of coal for the heart of her fire!

THE TRAIN THAT RAN OUT OF STEAM

Towards the end of the Second World War an unusual and tragic accident occurred in the townland of Straboe, Co Laois on 20 December 1944, where a train stalled because its engine had run out of steam. The Night Mail train from Dublin to Cork, heavily loaded in the pre-Christmas period with mails, passengers and perishable goods, crashed into the rear of a stationary cattle train causing much destruction and the death of a Post Office official who was sorting mail in the third postal van. The accident was also a most unfortunate occurrence for the Great Southern Railways (GSR), for it was the only accident in that company's history that caused a loss of life of a non-railway person. Just eleven days after the accident, the GSR went out of existence and its railways were taken over by Córas Iompair Éireann(CIÉ), newly-established under the Transport Act 1944.

Railways in Ireland suffered greatly from fuel shortages during the Second World War, which was officially referred to in this country as The Emergency. Locomotive coal was particularly difficult to obtain and the GSR reserved the best coal available for engines of passenger trains, especially the important Mail Trains and trains conveying perishable goods. However, the best coal was not always good and frequently it consisted of poor quality briquettes, ovoids and slack. The engines of goods, cattle and other special trains were allocated the remaining stocks of coal, which often were no better than slack and briquette dust held together by pitch and tar. This low-grade fuel formed clinker in engine fireboxes and had to be broken up by hand tools and removed from the firebox with hand shovels when steam pressure dropped. Clearing the firebox often took a lot of time, especially with the larger engines. Those who had to travel long journeys during The Emergency will remember being stopped for lengthy periods at stations while the engine firebox was being emptied of clinker, a fresh fire set, lighted and built up, before steam pressure could be raised sufficiently to enable the engine to restart its train. It was the loss of steam pressure in the engine of the cattle train that caused it to stall midway between Portarlington and Maryborough (now Portlaoise) on that fateful night of 20 December 1944.

Portarlington/*Cúil an tSúdaire* was and still is an important interchange point on the Dublin-Cork mainline, where traffic passes between the south and the west of Ireland. At the time of the accident, it was a common practice for rail vehicles from the Galway and Westport lines intended for destinations south of Portarlington to be attached to southbound trains at that station. The Night Mail was one of these trains and the operations of interchange involved shunting movements under the protection of the station's signals. The Night Mail trains on the Dublin-Cork line were usually heavy as, in addition to mail, they carried parcels, perishables and passengers. In 1944 there were very few passenger trains and the few carriages attached to the Night Mails tended to be crowded, or even overloaded in the pre-Christmas period. These mail trains were very long and frequently exceeded the full length of station platforms. To enable traffic from all vehicles to be handled at the platform, the train would have to pull forward and stop a second time to allow access to the rearmost vehicles. This enforced re-pulling by the Night Mail at Portarlington was a major contributory factor to the fatal accident that ensued.

The Night Mail
On 20 December 1944 the Dublin-Cork Night Mail consisted of 4-6-0 engine No 406 with coal tender, followed by three Post Office sorting vehicles, two passenger coaches, two Post Office parcels vans, eight other goods vans, three fish vans and three meat vans – a heavy train of 21 laden

A typical Dublin-Cork night mail train hauled by 2-6-0 engine No 372. Note the postal sorting vans next to the engine.

vehicles. The train weighed about 546 tons and was fitted with the continuous vacuum brake throughout. When it arrived at Portarlington at 10.45 p.m. the loading and unloading of mail, parcels and other goods took place for some ten minutes. When this work was done, a horsebox from the west of Ireland had to be attached to the rear of the train. Because of its length, the train even after re-pulling was still foul of the points leading to the siding at the Dublin end of the platform where the horsebox stood. Therefore, it was necessary for the Night Mail to pull further forward to allow the extra vehicle to be shunted out of the siding to the platform line and be attached to the end of the train. By drawing further forward from the platform the train had to pass the starter signal, which had been set at danger by the signalman because he had not yet received clearance from the next station that a preceding cattle train had already arrived there. At the subsequent inquiry, there was a direct conflict of evidence between the driver and fireman of the Night Mail on the one hand and the signalman on the other as to whether or not the starter and the advanced starter signals were actually at danger when the train was making the re-pull to enable the horsebox to be attached.

The Cattle Train
The cattle train consisted of 0-6-0 engine No 184 with coal tender, hauling 25 laden wagons and a guard's van. The train weighed about 345 tons and its load mainly was cattle from the Dublin markets bound for the meat factory at Roscrea, as well as some wagons of sundry goods. It had left Dublin at 3.30 p.m. in the afternoon but had encountered difficulties from the outset. On reaching Sallins only 29 kilometres from Dublin the fire had to be cleaned out and restarted because of the poor quality of coal. When the train was able to resume its journey, further stops were needed at Newbridge, Kildare and Monastereven to allow steam pressure in the engine's boiler to be built up to a level that would enable the train to proceed. It was 9.25 p.m. before Portarlington was reached – a distance of 65 kilometres from Dublin. Here the fire had to be cleaned again.

The 'fire-dropper' at Portarlington John Cunningham gave evidence later that the fire he cleaned 'was very bad and dirty', but when the cattle train had left at 10.10 p.m. the fire 'was good and steam pressure of 150lb was raised'. Nevertheless, the cattle train ground to a stop once more only five kilometres south of Portarlington. The driver, Dominick Lipper, gave evidence that steam pressure had dropped so low that he had to wait seven minutes for the pressure to be built up again to 150lb. The train continued for another five kilometres to Straboe, where falling steam pressure again compelled it to stop. On this occasion, pressure could not be built up and the driver decided

4-6-0 engine No 406 being lifted back on the track at Straboe after the Night Mail crashed into a cattle train on 20 December 1944.

Carcasses of cattle litter the field after the Night Mail crashed into the cattle train at Straboe.

to have the fire cleaned again. Driver Lipper said he was about 30 minutes stopped at Straboe, but steam pressure had not been sufficiently restored when the collision took place. Evidence was later given that the fuel resources of engine No 184 consisted of six hundredweight of coal briquettes and about 25 hundredweight of coal dust.

The Accident

The collision happened in total darkness in the townland of Straboe some nine kilometres south of Portarlington at about 11.25 p.m. and it caused great destruction. The Night Mail crashed into the rear of the cattle train with such force that eight wagons were almost totally destroyed, over 50 cattle killed and their carcasses strewn over lands on both sides of the line. The heavy 4-6-0 engine No 406 left the rails and fell on its side in a bog alongside the railway. Three of the leading postal vehicles were so severely damaged that they had to be withdrawn from service. As already noted, a postal sorter, Francis Devine, working in the third vehicle was killed and a number of others including the guard of the cattle train, Patrick Ferriter, were badly injured. What prevented greater destruction and loss of life was the fact that the fourth vehicle of the Night Mail was a pre-war steel passenger coach that withstood the impact and saved the following coach and goods vehicles from significant damage. In the circumstances, it could be argued that overall damage was comparatively light despite the unfortunate loss of a life and the heavy toll of cattle killed.

Statutory Inquiry

By order of the Minister for Industry & Commerce a formal investigation into the causes of the accident was held in January 1945 by the Railway Inspecting Officer Mr T. C. Courtney (who later became Chairman of CIÉ). The inquiry focused on the signals at Portarlington that allowed the Night Mail to leave, despite knowledge of the preceding cattle train, and the steps taken at Straboe to protect that train when it stalled because of fuel difficulties. Joseph Rosney, the station foreman on duty at Portarlington on the fateful night, agreed in evidence that he had instructed the driver of the Night Mail to bring his train forward some 120 metres beyond the station platform to facilitate the attaching of the horsebox. The driver, James Creegan, corroborated by his fireman, Patrick Leonard, had said to the foreman, 'The signal is against me,' but the foreman replied, 'I think you have the road.' Foreman Rosney told the inquiry that he thought he saw green light through the steam when he instructed Driver Creegan, but when he went back about two coach-lengths and as the train moved out he saw the starting signal showing red. James Maguire, the signalman on duty that night, swore that although he knew the Night Mail would have to move forward to allow the attaching of the horsebox, he did not at any time lower the starting signal to show a green light. His evidence was corroborated by two non-railway witnesses who had been standing on the road overbridge at Portarlington station that evening from the time of arrival until the time of departure of the Night Mail. The Signalman agreed, however, that it was customary at Portarlington to allow trains to pass the starting signal at danger for shunting movements, even though this was against the rules.

With regard to the cattle train that had preceded the Night Mail, Foreman Rosney said the guard's van at its rear showed a red tail lamp and one white sidelight when leaving Portarlington. Driver Creegan stated, however, that on approaching Straboe he saw ahead only a white light to his right, which he took to be that of a train approaching on the up line from Cork. He did not see any red light until he had almost met the rear of the stalled train and, although he at once shut off steam and applied his brakes, the crash occurred within seconds. The cattle train was driven forward about 20 metres by the impact. In normal practice an engine driver approaching the rear of a stationary goods train should have seen three red lights ahead – the red tail lamp on the back of the brake van as well as two red lights, one on each side of the van. The latter were made to show a white light ahead to indicate to the driver that his train was complete and, by adding a red glass slide, to show a red light to the rear. But this cattle train on the night of 20 December had only one white sidelight and, as it had no red glass slide, it was showing white to both front and rear. Its red tail lamp was showing a weak light due to the shortage of paraffin oil. It was a sad reflection on railway practice during The Emergency that, due to scarcity of oil and materials, there was a tendency to reduce the number of lamps carried on trains in order to make the best use of the limited supplies of paraffin oil available.

At the inquiry the guard of the cattle train Patrick Ferriter found it hard to recall what happened as he had been traumatised by the impact. He agreed, however, that he had only one sidelight instead of two and explained he had no red slide for that light, but did have the proper red tail lamp at the back of his van. Guard Ferriter said it had often been the case that only two lamps would be issued to a guard. When asked why he had not protected his stationary train in accordance with the normal practice (placing one detonator on the track 440 yards behind, a second detonator 880 yards behind and three further detonators 1,320 yards behind the train), he asserted that the cattle train had just begun to move off when the Night Mail had collided with it. However the engine crew denied this, stating that the cattle train was still stationary at the moment of impact. Asked specifically why he had not protected the train with detonators Guard Ferriter replied

Heavy cranes try to lift Night Mail engine No 406 out of the field after it crashed at Straboe.

that at the previous stop he had nearly been left behind when the train restarted and he had thought on this occasion that the stop would be brief.

The official report of the Railways Inspecting Officer published in March 1945 found that the primary cause of the accident was the failure of Driver Creegan and Fireman Leonard of the Night Mail to observe and obey the advanced starter signal at Portarlington. The secondary cause was the failure of Guard Ferriter to protect the cattle train in accordance with the regulations when it was stopped by fuel difficulties at Straboe. Arising out of the evidence, it was recommended that the regulations regarding rear lighting of goods and cattle trains be strictly enforced and, if the number of lights had to be reduced due to the shortage of paraffin oil, a suitable amendment of the regulations should be made.

Criminal Trial

A criminal trial of the persons held to be responsible for the accident followed in August 1945, when three railway men were charged with unlawfully killing Francis Devine and, by willful omission and neglect, endangering the safety of passengers being conveyed on the railway. The trial opened in the Central Criminal Court Dublin on 11 December 1945 before Judge Shannon. All of the three accused, Driver Creegan, Fireman Leonard and Guard Ferriter, pleaded not guilty. Having heard evidence similar to that presented at the Railways Inspecting Officer's inquiry, the jury after an hour's absence found that Driver Creegan and Fireman Leonard were not guilty on both charges and they were set free. Guard Ferriter was found not guilty on the first charge of manslaughter, but guilty on the second charge of endangering the safety of passengers. He was given a sentence of nine months' imprisonment, but for medical reasons this was suspended. Guard Ferriter had been badly injured in the accident and, if the sentence were to be imposed, it would have to be served in a prison hospital. As the judge felt that Patrick Ferriter's health had been completely shattered as a result of the collision, he decided to suspend the prison sentence.

Aftermath

CIÉ had taken over the GSR since 1 January 1945 and, in the light of what had transpired since the accident, decided to make significant changes to the signalling at Portarlington. Colour-light repeater signals were installed on the left-hand (or driver's) side of the track at the south end of the station and much of the trackwork was remodelled. All down line semaphore signals and some of the up line ones were replaced by colour-light signals and both the Down Starter and Advanced Starter signals were repositioned on the driver's side of the main line.

The Ballycastle-Ballymoney train stuck in a snowdrift after the blizzard of March 1947.

the train was now truly trapped in a deep snowdrift. Driver Limerick continued:

> Then I couldn't get back, with that much snow around the brake van, or I'd have put the brake van off the road. We were lucky enough, for there was a farmhouse just beside us – Delargy they called them – and Jim Delargy came across to see how many passengers there were. He brought across a bag of bread and a great big buttermilk can of tea and as many cups as he could carry.
>
> We stayed there all that night, with the passengers huddled in the van. There was a fire in the van at first, but it was briquette coal. Now briquettes burn all right in the engine with a draught, but there was no draught in the van. So we tried to burn the briquettes as best we could and kept poking at them. But the more we poked, the more they went out.

The next morning a relief train from Ballycastle managed to get through to the snowbound train and took off the passengers, bringing them back to the starting point of their journey a day after they left it. The engine crew and guard stayed with the snowbound train all that day, with their engine still embedded in a two-metre drift. The second night out they spent in Delargy's house, sitting in the farm kitchen around the turf fire while draughts from the blizzard outside crept under the half doors. On the third day about a hundred men were recruited from the local labour exchange in Ballycastle and dispatched to dig the snow out of the cutting. After many hours work, the engine and its train were finally freed at 3 p.m. on 14 March, just as the dusk was gathering at the end of their third day snowbound in North Antrim.

BY TRAIN TO TRAMORE

The seaside resort of Tramore/ *Trá Mhór*, some eleven kilometres south of Waterford/ *Port Láirge*, could only be reached by train along a single-track self-contained broad gauge railway that was completely isolated from the rest of the Irish railway system. Its Waterford terminus was at Railway Square off Manor Street in the south of the city, some three kilometres from the main railway station on the north bank of the River Suir. Many of the engines, carriages and practices of the Tramore Line were unique in the history of Irish railways and its closure at the end of January 1960 was most strongly resented by the citizens of Waterford.

Perhaps the most endearing characteristic of the Tramore Line was the independence of spirit that pervaded its entire operation. The staff worked most efficiently in their own way and never showed much interest in 'the big railway on the other side of the Suir'. To catch a train from either Waterford Manor or Tramore was like rushing to Mass on Sundays, for a large bell suspended from a high pole in the station was rung loudly five minutes before departure to hurry the customers along and it was rung again just before the train left. Regular users of the line always seemed to wait for 'the five-minute bell' before rushing off to the station. Because of its isolation, the Tramore Line had retained, longer than any other railway in Ireland or Britain, the oldest working engines and carriages. From their introduction in 1855 until the last one fell victim to a strange accident in 1935, three 2-2-2 single-drive tank engines built by Fairbairns of Leeds of the type seen in engravings of the earliest trains had worked the Tramore line. These engines hauled ancient carriages with full sides and windows only on their east side facing the prevailing winds from the sea. Doors were only provided on the west side of the carriages as the platforms at both termini were on that side of the line, which had no intermediate stations. To add to their incongruous appearance, these ancient carriages had only waist-high sides to facilitate the checking of tickets from the platforms. In cold or wet weather, travel in these carriages must have been quite unpleasant.

An old 2-2-2 engine built in 1855 for the Waterford & Tramore Railway leaving Waterford Manor with a train for Tramore in the 1930s.

The Tramore Line was also unique in other ways. It had no signal cabins and just one signal protecting the only level crossing on the railway at Bath Street, which was opened and closed by the porter on duty at Waterford Manor. Unique marketing practices were also used and these were often ahead of their time. To attract custom to the early morning trains, 'Bathers Excursion' tickets were sold to entice Waterford citizens to travel to Tramore for an early morning swim. The tickets were only valid, however, until 9 a.m. to ensure that all who bought them would return to Waterford to do a full day's work. 'Atlantic Dance' tickets, which included admission to the Atlantic Ballroom in Tramore were issued after 8 p.m. to encourage patronage of the lightly-filled evening trains. These tickets, which were enormously popular, were valid for return on a 3 a.m. special from Tramore that brought the dancers home to the city and encouraged many a romance to blossom in the darkened carriages of that train. But the most unique practice of all on the line was that members of all religious orders in Waterford were permitted to travel free on the railway at all times. This custom no doubt generated much goodwill for the Tramore line from the people of Waterford and also explains why such resentment was felt when that old and unique institution was finally closed on 31 January 1960.

The first serious accident on the line occurred on 24 August 1935 when the 12.15 p.m. to Tramore hauled by 2-2-2 tank engine No 483 met with disaster. The day was sunny and warm and the train was crowded. The engine had recently been overhauled and was in sprightly form travelling at 35mph, when suddenly near Carricklong Bridge the engine left the rails dragging two coaches with it down the embankment. There were a number of injuries to passengers, but none as serious as those suffered by the engine crew, Driver Mick Power and Fireman Michael Phelan. The driver had injuries to his neck and back and the fireman had a broken collarbone and serious burns. Both men spent nearly a year in hospital. The cause of this mishap was never clearly established, but the railway men claimed that it was an act of sabotage by a group known as 'The Blueshirts', a vaguely fascist movement in the 1930s that defended large-farmer interests. The only fatality of the sabotage was engine No 483, the last remaining single-drive tank locomotive in either Ireland or Britain. This engine should have had another fifteen years of life left and was intended for preservation, but because of the damage caused to it in the mishap at Carricklong, a decision was taken to cut it up for scrap the following year.

The second and more sensational accident happened on 13 August 1947 to the 11.15 p.m. train from Waterford, hauled by former Midland & Great Western Railway 0-6-0 tank engine No 560 with seven coaches and 23 passengers, which was crewed by Driver Jim Doolan and Fireman Tom Colfer. Running down the moderate incline of 1 in 140 on the approach to Tramore, the brake failed to hold the train – the first-ever such failure on the

Engine No 560 on Strand Road, Tramore on 14 August 1947 having crashed through station buffers .

line. The driver frantically reversed the engine while the fireman opened the sand-lever and the cylinder cocks, but all to no avail. The train continued through the terminus and plunged through the outer station wall. Engine No 560 landed upright on all wheels on the roadway, with its buffers almost touching the steps of the Hotel De Luxe. Miraculously, nobody was injured. But No 560 sat in splendour for over 50 hours blocking the main road to the 'Big Strand' and providing the main attraction to visitors during the 'Fifteenth of August Holiday' until it was finally hauled back to the rails in the early morning of 16 August 1947.

THE MAYOR'S OUTING

In 1928 the local businessmen and Waterford Corporation began a yearly outing for deprived children to Tramore and the railway coped admirably with this mass exodus until the custom came to an end in 1944. The significance of this event, which was known as the 'Poor Children's Outing', was well illustrated in the following extract from the *Waterford News* in September 1930:

> On Wednesday last, 1700 children assembled in the Courthouse grounds and were formed into groups, each child being given a piece of cardboard on which was recorded his or her name and address. This was then secured to the child's clothing by a safety pin.
>
> At 9.30 a.m. the children moved in groups out into Catherine Street and formed up behind the Barrack Street Brass and Reed Band and, headed by the Mayor and Corporation in their robes of office, the procession marched into Parnell Street and on to Manor Street station, where a special train waited.
>
> Promptly at 10.30 a.m. the heavily laden train with its excited and noisy passengers headed for Tramore, the Mayor and other officials occupying a special carriage behind the engine. During the day the following items were consumed:
>
> 40lb Ham; 282 Long Pans; 1750 Rock Buns; 1100 Currant Buns; 40 Tins of Sweets; 86lb Butter; 92lb Jam; 3300 Apples; 1200 Bananas; 5 boxes Foreign Apples; 138 dozen Small Minerals; 136 dozen Large Minerals; 7 stone Sugar; 16lb Tea; 40 gallons Milk; 1670 Meat Sandwiches; and 1630 Butter and Jam Sandwiches.

The happy children were returned home on a special train at 8.30 p.m. in the evening.

CAHIR VIADUCT DISASTER

Around 4.30 a.m. on the morning of 21 December 1955 a horrific accident occurred at Cahir/*An Chathair*, Co Tipperary, when a runaway, loose-coupled and fully-laden beet train bound for Thurles Sugar Factory demolished a buffer-block, crashed through the cross girders of the adjoining viaduct and plunged through the bridge into the River Suir some 13 metres below. The 2-6-0 Woolwich engine No 375 with its coal tender and 22 wagons of beet fell off the bridge and were wrecked, killing instantly the driver, Cornelius Kelly, and the fireman, Francis Frahill. Both men from Limerick had been footplate mates for 42 trips in 1955 and had long experience of the powerful Woolwich locomotives. Their apparent loss of

A view of Cahir station platform in April 1955.

control of the heavy beet train on its descent into Cahir that night is still a mystery and is a cause of great sadness to all railwaymen.

The special beet train was scheduled to operate daily during the sugar beet campaign from Bridgetown in Co Wexford to the sugar factory in Thurles, travelling over the single-track Waterford-Limerick main line via Clonmel, Cahir and Limerick Junction. The train consisted of 32 laden beet wagons and a 20-ton guard's van hauled by the 100-ton engine and tender, giving a total train weight of about 560 tons. Its overall length was 230 metres, somewhat in excess of the length of the passing loops at Cahir. Because of the late running of trains on the Waterford-Limerick line that night, the special beet train was due to cross the Limerick-Waterford Night Mail at Cahir rather than Clonmel, as would happen normally. This unusual crossing place was probably a contributing factor to the horrific disaster that ensued.

The Night Mail from Limerick reached Cahir first at 4.22 a.m. and stopped at the platform beside the water-column to enable the steam engine to replenish its water tank. In stopping there the tail of the 130 metre train extended back towards the viaduct it had just crossed and blocked the points leading from the crossing loop at the Limerick end of the station. This prevented any train coming from the Clonmel direction and using the crossing loop from rejoining the main line as it continued across the viaduct towards Limerick. To protect the stationary Night Mail, the signalman placed the signals from the Clonmel direction at danger and changed the points at the Limerick end of the loop to face into a 40 metre siding that ended with a buffer-block just short of the eastern abutment of Cahir Viaduct. It had been the signalman's intention, once the beet special had been stopped by the signals outside the station, to allow it to move forward with caution into the loop and continue into the siding until the tail of the train had cleared the loop points at the Clonmel end of the station, thus allowing the Night Mail to continue its journey to Waterford.

The Disaster

The Mail had been at the water-column for a few minutes when the shrieking whistle of the beet special was heard approaching the station. Most of the witnesses said they heard several short blasts of the whistle, but Driver John Terry of the Night Mail asserted at the subsequent inquiry that there was one continuous blast. The beet special was travelling fast at speeds estimated between 35 and 45mph and sparks were seen flying from the wheels and brake-blocks, indicating that the engine brakes were applied. No steam was observed coming from the engine or on the footplate. Fireman Thomas Murphy of the Night Mail said that, as engine No 375 passed him, he saw the driver and fireman and they appeared quite calm: 'They were just

A view showing the hole (at centre left) through which the beet special fell into the River Suir at Cahir on 21 December 1955.

Wrecked wagons of sugar beet lying beneath Cahir Viaduct.

the same as if nothing was going to happen.' Then a great crash was heard as No 375 collided with the buffer-block and 'then the forward wagons seemed to rebound and then go on again with a chuck'. The rear portion of the beet special stopped with the guard's van close to the van of the Mail.

Although the night was dark, the weather at the time of the disaster was described as fine, clear and dry. The guard of the beet special, William Grant from Waterford, survived the crash and was not seriously injured. He described to an *Evening Press* reporter his reaction to hearing the crash as the engine hit the buffer-block:

> Then I saw it was going over the bridge into the river. I got a terrible shock. I'm not over it yet. I was preparing to jump when the coupling broke after the loco and twenty-two of the wagons had gone down. That left ten wagons and the van in which I was on the line.
>
> There was a terrible smash as the whole lot went toppling down a drop of about forty feet. Only the nose of the engine went into the water. But the tender telescoped into it and the dead driver and fireman were still in it. The wagons piled up all around, but none of them went on top of the engine. The beet was scattered in piles all over the place.

One of the few people living in new houses near the railway to have heard any unusual sound was Garda Thomas Delaney who was awakened by what he described as 'a fierce tearing noise'. He said he got up and looked out towards the railway viaduct but could see nothing. But he felt something had gone wrong and almost immediately afterwards he was called out to the disaster scene.

Mrs Josephine Richardson, wife of the station master at Cahir who lived in the station house, told an *Irish Press* reporter:

> I heard the distress signal whistling and the brakes screeching. I knew there was danger but heard no crash. I heard a knock on the window and Tom Walsh the signalman saying there had been a terrible crash. My husband rushed out. I got a bottle of holy water and a blessed candle and rushed to the scene with my little daughter Anne. We searched the wreckage in case any of the crew had jumped but found no one. I sprinkled holy water on the wreckage from the bridge and we prayed.

Rescue Attempts

Fire brigade men, gardaí and railwaymen were quick to reach the scene of the crash, but the low-level site beneath the viaduct presented problems. Fire Officer Thomas Kirrane of the Cahir Fire Brigade described the scene to an *Evening Herald* reporter:

> It was dark when we arrived on the scene, but we could discern railway

wagons piled up with the aid of torches. We immediately set about getting electric light and we ran a lead from the railway station down to the scene of the crash. But the distance was too long and all the lights fused. Eventually we succeeded in getting light by connecting up with a nearby house. Before the light came, we had been groping around in the dark looking for some sign of the missing driver and fireman, but they were not discovered for about fifteen or twenty minutes.

The search started along the riverbank because we thought that they would have either fallen or jumped from the engine. But then, standing on the bank, I could see the engine driver still at his post and standing upright, but he appeared to be dead and badly injured. I could see no sign of the fireman, but there was a hand sticking up out of the wreckage near where the driver was. The engine was lying in about sixteen feet of water, which was boiling around it. There was a lot of steam.

Railway rescue workers made several attempts to release the bodies by hauling the tender off the engine by means of a steel hawser attached to the coal tender and towed by an engine on the railway line above. But the hawser broke repeatedly under the strain and the effort was abandoned. The fireman's body was recovered after about nine hours of work by a CIÉ breakdown crew, who succeeded in reaching it from the riverbank and bringing it ashore. The body of the driver was not recovered until 9.30 p.m., some seventeen hours after the crash, by a team of oxy-acetylene workers brought in from the Hammond Lane Foundry in Dublin. The final rescue operations were carried out at considerable danger to the workers themselves, as the wrecked tender was continually settling further on to the engine.

Examination of Wreckage
After crashing through the floor and cross-girders of the viaduct, engine No 375 came to rest on the bank of the River Suir in an upright position, but at an angle of about thirty degrees. Its leading pony-truck wheels were about 2.5 metres under water and the footplate was resting on the bank. Any examination, therefore, had to be done under conditions of extreme difficulty and took considerable time. To extricate the bodies of the driver and fireman, it was necessary to cut away much of the cab, to cut off the regulator handle and to remove the brake control and some other fittings. Because of this, it was impossible to be quite certain about the position of the brake gear at the time of the accident. Examination disclosed no defects in the brake gear, or any which would be likely to cause or contribute to cause the accident. Certain parts were found broken or otherwise damaged, but these deficiencies were apparently caused by the accident. The position of the

Wrecked wagons of beet beneath Cahir Viaduct.

brake controls at the time of the accident could not be ascertained.

The tender was found lying on a cross-wall between two of the piers of the viaduct. Its front-end was crushed into the engine cab and it was very badly damaged. The screw-gear for hand operation of the tender brakes was found in the 'on' position and the brake gear was severely damaged, but careful examination disclosed no defects that might have rendered the brakes ineffective. One brake-block was considerably worn, but this in itself would not have interfered with the operation of the brakes. The vacuum brake's operating gear was in order as far as could be seen, but the condition of the piston rods suggested that the vacuum brake had not been operated for some time before the accident. The brake on the guard's van was found to be in good order. At the subsequent public inquiry CIÉ engineers affirmed that engine No 375 was maintained above the average goods special standard and that there was nothing in all the repairs to the engine that would cause it to go out of order.

Test Train

Following the disaster, a test train was run over the line from Clonmel to Cahir on 18 January 1956 with a train similar to that involved in the crash, but weighing 30 tons more and with a similar Woolwich 2-6-0 engine. Between Clonmel and Cahir the railway crosses a ridge of high ground, the highest point of which is at Nicholastown level crossing about eight kilometres from Cahir. From this point the line falls for a while before rising moderately at an average gradient of 1 in 370 to reach a point some four kilometres from Cahir. The line then falls continuously at a gradient of 1 in 152 to the Cahir distant signal and from there undulates slightly before reaching the station. These gradients are not excessively steep and, provided care is taken to keep a train under control on the long downward slope into Cahir, there should have been no difficulty about stopping at the home signal, as was required of the beet special in the early morning of 21 December 1955.

On the test run, the maximum speed attained was 33mph at a point six kilometres from Cahir. Here steam was shut off and speed reduced on entering the falling gradient of 1 in 152. At a point four kilometres from the buffer-block the speed was 25mph, with the tender and van brakes applied intermittently. Near the Cahir distant signal at 15mph, the tender brake was released and the van brake eased. It was found necessary to apply steam on the slight up grade near the home signal to bring the train into the station.

Statutory Inquiry

By order of the Minister for Industry & Commerce an inquiry into the accident was held in Dublin by the Railways Inspecting Officer, Mr T. L. Hogan, on 15-17 February 1956. In his official report published on 25 April, Mr Hogan gave it as his considered opinion that the accident had been caused by the beet special being out of control when approaching and passing through Cahir station. He could find no explanation for the occurrence other than that the driver failed to keep his train under control and obey signals. Action to stop the train had not been initiated by the driver until the train was entering the station, by which time it was too late to be effective.

The report stated that the guard did not observe the Cahir distant signal and apparently did not look out for the home signal until the driver whistled, when the engine was close to that signal and travelling at high speed. At this whistle, the guard had applied his handbrake partially but did not put it on fully until the van was passing the signal cabin, by which time the engine was close to the point of impact. The Railways Inspecting Officer considered that the guard had not been keeping a good look out as required by the rules and that he was slow to appreciate the situation and apply his brake fully.

An aerial view of the steaming engine of the beet special with its nose in the River Suir.

However, in spite of this, the officer did not believe that the outcome would have been affected even if the van brake had been applied to the full when the driver whistled.

Criticism was levelled in the official report at the layout of Cahir station and about the operation of signals at the time of the accident. While it did not lead to, or excuse, the passing of a home signal at high speed and could not be regarded as the cause of the accident, the Inspecting Officer nevertheless thought that the operation of signals at Cahir was irregular. The down Night Mail from Limerick was brought into the up platform line and the up beet special from Waterford was brought into the down platform line. This was done without the provision or operation of two-way signalling. This practice was a matter of convenience for the loading and unloading of mails and perishable goods, but many undesirable effects resulted including the signalman having to leave his cabin to bring in trains by the use of hand signals. Had the proper loops been used on the night of the accident, the driver of the beet special would have been presented with the same signal indications as were in fact exhibited. The Railways Inspecting Officer recommended that the practice of using either of the up or down loops at Cahir for trains running in the opposite direction should cease, unless double-way signalling could be installed for the control of such irregular movements. In the event, two-way signalling was installed at Cahir in March 1957 as a direct result of the Railways Inspecting Officer's recommendation.

What Exactly Did Happen?
In an accident such as this in which the engine crew perished, it will never be possible to know for certain what happened to cause the beet special to become a runaway train. Was either man on the footplate of engine No 375 taken ill? From all the evidence at the inquiry, it does not seem so. Both men were seen to be quite calm at the controls just before the crash. Could they have mistaken their position on approaching Cahir? This seems unlikely as the engine whistle would indicate that they knew their train was approaching the station out of control. A possible explanation for what happened may be that the engine crew of No 375 felt that the train would either plough into the ballast and come to a stop before reaching the viaduct, or would be diverted back on to the main line at the Limerick end of the station loop. But in either case, they were so preoccupied with the task of stopping the runaway train that they had only a very short time to take action. Unfortunately, it was too late for any sort of effective action by the time their train had reached Cahir station.

The powerful Woolwich 2-6-0 locomotive No 375 lay where it had fallen on the bed of the River Suir for over seven weeks while a decision was awaited on its future. Eventually, on 11 February 1956 this fine engine was cut up and removed for scrap, as it was considered to be beyond repair. It was a sad final chapter to this tragic story that has puzzled railwaymen for many years. They believe that there was something strange and inexplicable about this last major accident with a steam engine on the CIÉ system.

THE CLOGH BRIDGE ACCIDENT

Around 9.30 a.m. on New Year's Eve 1975 an excavator on the back of a lorry struck at Clogh Bridge, some five kilometres south of Gorey/*Guaire* station in Co Wexford, dislodged its granite masonry and buckled the railway just minutes before the 8.05 a.m. Rosslare Harbour-Dublin train was due. In spite of frantic efforts to stop the train, it hit the bridge at an estimated 60mph causing a terrible accident in which five people were killed and thirty injured. It was the worst rail crash in CIÉ's history until that time.

The casualty figures would have been considerably higher only that the first two carriages were closed and empty, as they had been intended for use by passengers joining the train further along the line. These leading vehicles, as well as a luggage van were completely shattered when the train jumped the rails at the damaged bridge. Most of the injured were in the third carriage, but five people were killed in the fourth carriage when it was penetrated by the coach behind it and came to rest spanning the gap in the line. Driver Joseph O'Neill of Rosslare Harbour, who had been in the left-hand seat of engine No B132, had a miraculous escape. Deeply shocked and with a back injury, he managed to crawl out after his engine overturned and tumbled down an embankment into a field.

Christy Hill, a local man, was driving his car nearby when he was stopped by the lorry driver and told the bridge had been damaged. Almost simultaneously he heard a train siren in the distance. Describing how he ran through a field and up on to the railway embankment to a point about 50 metres from the buckled rails, Christy Hill continued:

> I waved frantically at the driver to stop. But the driver blew for me to get out of the way and I could then hear the brakes going on. I ran to my house but the phone was not working. I managed to get a phone that did work and rang the gardaí in Gorey.

Rescue work began at once in bad conditions of heavy rain. A fleet of ambulances, doctors and nurses, fire brigade personnel, gardaí and volunteer

Wreckage fallen through Clogh Bridge, Co Wexford, 31 December 1975.

workers converged on the scene from Gorey, Enniscorthy and Wexford, but they had a very difficult task in disentangling the wreckage. The impact had been extremely severe, coach bodies being smashed and wheel-bogies and underframes badly twisted. Rescuers had to spend about two hours trying to extricate the dead and the injured from the wreckage. Volunteer helpers who earned high praise included County Council staff, mechanics from garages in the area and people from various businesses throughout North Wexford.

The Chairman of CIÉ, Dr Liam St John Devlin, expressed his shock and deep grief at the tragic accident and thanked the various emergency services for their wonderful work and dedication. He paid particular tribute to the local people who unselfishly gave assistance at the scene of the accident.

Damage caused to railway underbridges by excessively high loads on road vehicles has unfortunately become an increasingly frequent phenomenon over the last three decades. Many railway bridges throughout the country have been damaged to varying degrees and, in the cases of repeated damage, Iarnród Éireann in co-operation with relevant local authorities have had bridges raised and roads lowered so as to minimise the risks of future accidents of this kind. Thanks to this action and to greater vigilance on the part of railway staff, no other comparable serious incident caused by bridge dislodgment has occurred since that tragic accident at Clogh Bridge in 1975.

Derailed engine No B132 and wrecked carriages at Clogh Bridge, Co Wexford.

DISTRESS IN DALKEY

Great distress, but thankfully no loss of life, resulted from a severe crash between two crowded commuter trains in the Khyber Pass Tunnel just east of Dalkey/*Deilginis* station on the Bray-Dublin suburban line on the very frosty Friday morning of 16 November 1979. The force of the impact was such that it drove the stationary first train forward by some 40 metres and resulted in 36 people being injured, eight of them seriously. The driver of the second train from Bray that embedded itself in the rear of the preceding train, was trapped in his cab for over three hours before he could be freed and flown by helicopter to St Vincent's Hospital, Dublin.

The crash took place at a most inaccessible point between Killiney and Dalkey stations. While the point of collision was some eight metres inside the tunnel from the Dalkey end, the wreckage piled up outside where the ground slopes close to the perpendicular on both sides of the track for some 25 metres. Rescuers had either to make the tricky descent through trees and heavy undergrowth or walk along the tracks from Dalkey station some 300 metres to the west. Both trains were crowded with commuters, including many students and school children, and local people reaching the scene found twisted metal, schoolbags, briefcases and morning newspapers sodden in blood littering the tracks. Passengers had been catapulted from their seats and many of them were thrown through windows and doors by the impact. School children got the worst of the impact, as most of them were in the two rear carriages of the first train.

The Dublin Emergency Plan was put into operation as soon as word of the crash broke about 8.40 a.m. Air Corps helicopters took off from the helipad at St Vincent's Hospital, Elm Park, carrying medical teams and supplies. They landed in the grounds of a house near the scene of the crash as the injured were taken from the trains and laid on carriage seats on the tracks. A permanent way trolley was pushed up the tracks from Dalkey station and used to carry stretchers with the casualties back to the station where a fleet of ambulances awaited to take them to three of the nearest

A view of crashed coaches at the mouth of the Kyber Pass Tunnel, Dalkey on 16 November 1979.

hospitals at Loughlinstown, Dún Laoghaire and Merrion. Local people brought blankets, tea and coffee for the less seriously injured as they queued for ambulances. Three helicopters were used to ferry the more seriously injured to St Vincent's Hospital. A local medical practitioner, Dr Neal Webb, broke a leg while trying to get down the steep embankment to the crash scene and had to be taken to hospital with the crash victims.

Local residents, Robert Fowler and his wife Phillippa living on Sorrento Road, saw the crash take place while getting ready to leave their home that morning. Both rushed down the embankment to see what help they could give. Robert said:

I was in the bathroom shaving and wondered why the train had stopped for so long. A few seconds later the other train came from behind and I could see the carriages rise up on the impact.

John Delahunt from Bray said he missed the 8.10 a.m. at Bray and took the 8.17 a.m. instead:

> I was sitting in one of the carriages near the front when the train stopped outside Dalkey. I didn't know what was wrong. The windows were misted up. Just as we began to clean them there was a tremendous thump. Everyone was thrown all over the place but the children at the back got off worst. There were people lying on the track bleeding and there was a lot of panic.

As this accident took place before the electrification of the Howth-Bray service in 1984, both trains involved were hauled by diesel engines. The 8.17 consisted of a diesel locomotive, a steam heating van and five passenger carriages. The 8.27 train from Bray was headed by locomotive 207 hauling a brake van, three passenger carriages and a heating van. No 207 came to rest with the twisted remains of the rearmost passenger carriage of the 8.17 embedded in its cab, trapping the driver who still had his hand on the brake lever when medical teams reached him three hours after the crash. The rear three passenger carriages of the 8.17 were very badly damaged, the rearmost being demolished, the second from the rear lifted from its bogies and telescoped into the next carriage. The body of the second bogie-less carriage was lifted high over the remains of the last carriage fouling the down track to Bray. This accident could well have been much more serious but for the fact that the morning Dublin-Rosslare Harbour express had just passed on the down track minutes before the crash occurred.

After the accident a CIÉ spokesman said that the first train came to a danger signal outside Dalkey and stopped. The second train should have been warned of this, but apparently it was not. In the case of a danger signal staying up and a train being kept waiting, a flagman goes down the track and guides the train through. The spokesman added, 'The flagman was on his way to do this when the crash took place.'

The subsequent official inquiry into the Dalkey accident was held on 15 April 1980 by Mr J. V. Feehan, Inspecting Officer of Railways. He concluded that the accident was caused by the 8.27 a.m. train from Bray moving at such speed that its driver, when he became aware of an obstruction on the line ahead, could not stop his train before it collided with the rear of the 8.17 a.m. train which was stationary outside the Dalkey Up Outer Home signal. He added that it was probable that the 8.27 a.m. train had departed from Killiney station while the Up Starting signal at that station was still displaying a danger

A breakdown crane attempting to clear wreckage after the Dalkey accident.

aspect and that subsequently it was running at a speed somewhat in excess of the 30mph maximum permitted in the published list of permanent speed restrictions that apply to the sharply curving line between Killiney and Dalkey stations.

THE BUTTEVANT DISASTER

The worst rail disaster in Ireland in the twentieth century occurred on Friday, 1 August 1980 when the 10 a.m. Dublin-Cork passenger train, passing at speed through Buttevant/*Cill an Mullach* station in north Co Cork around 12.45 p.m., left the rails and careered into an embankment causing the leading carriages to jack-knife across the double-track main line. Eighteen people, including the train guard and a pantry boy from the dining car, lost their lives and about seventy-five passengers received injuries of varying severity.

The Disaster

The scene of the disaster was described in *The Irish Times* the following day:

> Most of the dead and injured were in the first three carriages which became a mangled and grotesque-looking wreckage. The first carriage was actually compressed and flattened with gaping holes visible in the roof and floor areas. A number of the bodies were thrown through the floor on impact and these were the last of the dead to be recovered late last evening as huge cranes gently prised the coaches upwards allowing doctors and ambulance workers access. One of the bodies recovered last night was that of an infant.
>
> Although many of the injured were calling for help from inside the carriages, rescuers had great difficulty in reaching them because of the distorted layout of the wreckage. Among the first into the carriages from the rescue mission were the nurses from the County Hospital Mallow who reached the injured and the dying at great personal risk to themselves.

An English general practitioner, Dr Freda Naylor of Liverpool, who was a passenger on the train attended to many of the injured. She said they suffered from multiple and internal injuries. Her husband, a computer scientist Lesley Naylor, said the seriously injured were mainly men who were in the restaurant cars:

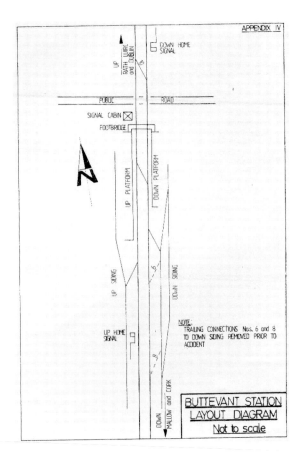

APPENDIX IV

Buttevant station
layout diagram.

It was lucky the call had not gone out for lunch or there would have been
more people dead. Breakfast had been late out of Dublin and only a few
had gone to the dining cars. That is where most of the casualties
occurred.

A sixteen-year-old student, Seán Kerrigan from Longford, was in the dining
car when the disaster happened:

I was sitting in the restaurant car at the front because there was nowhere
else. The train was crowded. My friend was down in the train
somewhere. Just as we were going into the station there was this terrible
skidding and screeching. It reminded me of a motor-bike going out of
control. Then there was this terrible crashing of metal and the whole
train was breaking up. But strangely, although the carriage was crowded,
I didn't hear any shrieking or shouting.

The carriage seemed to be all pressed together and I managed to get
through a broken window and climb out. The roof was all pressed in. I

198

Buttevant station after the disaster on 1 August 1980.

wonder how I survived. The only way I could get away from the wreckage was by walking along the roofs of the crashed carriages. They were all tilted over.

Seán Kerrigan said he estimated the train was travelling at about 60mph. It had slowed down some miles back for engineering works and it had been accelerating for about five minutes before the crash.

A fifteen-year-old Dublin student, Niamh Halpenny of Stillorgan, was on her way to France and she became separated from her baggage in the shambles. Some six hours later, her baggage turned up at the GAA Community Hall in Buttevant. Survivors of the crash paid tribute to the local people for the way in which they organised the scene, gathered up scattered baggage and handed over anything of value they found. Father Jim Murray of Skibbereen, who was on a visit home, tended to many of the seriously injured and dying and gave them the last rites. He paid special tribute to Mr and Mrs Donie Murphy of Cregane whose home was a short distance from the station. They gave sustenance and assistance to scores of survivors who were able to walk away from the scene of the crash.

A local councillor, Michael Broderick, was sitting in his car at the level crossing at Buttevant station when the disaster happened. He said that as the Dublin train approached the station, he saw another train coming up the other track against it:

> This train was sounding its hooter. I then saw Dinny Joe O'Sullivan in the signal box waving and shouting frantically. The next thing I heard was a loud bang. Then a lot of people screaming and I saw some coming out of the windows of the train. As I ran down the track, I saw three bodies. I helped pull a visitor from Brisbane out of one of the windows. I then rang Mary Hayes the assistant matron at Mallow County Hospital and within minutes the Cork County Disaster Plan had been put into effect and ambulances and doctors were on their way.

Fire brigades, ambulances and teams of doctors were arriving at the scene all afternoon and many of the townspeople of Butttevant, especially those living close to the station, turned their homes into improvised rescue centers. Later, helicopters began to land in a barley field near the crash scene bringing in more doctors and helping to remove the more seriously injured to hospital. The Minister for Transport, Albert Reynolds TD, also arrived by helicopter and said he had ordered a full public inquiry minutes after he heard the news of the disaster. He and the government were deeply saddened and shocked by the tragedy and extended their sympathies to the relatives of the dead or injured.

The Derailed Train

The 10 a.m. Dublin-Cork train on that Friday morning just before the August bank holiday weekend was a twelve-coach train hauled by 071 class engine No 075 and had an estimated tare weight of 461 tonnes. The coaches had screw-shackle connections between the vehicles. The engine and the first eight carriages were entirely derailed when the train was suddenly diverted through the turnout at the south end of the station into the goods yard. The ninth carriage came to rest with only its leading bogie wheels derailed and the last three vehicles did not leave the rails.

After the crash the trailing bogie wheels of engine No 075 were deeply embedded in the ballast of the siding near the southern turnout and still attached to the engine was a van that had lost its wheels, but whose steel body was still virtually intact. However, behind it the following three carriages – a first-class coach and two dining cars – were totally demolished. The under-frame of one of these vehicles landed upside-down nearly ten metres ahead of the locomotive. The next standard-class coach was very badly telescoped at its leading end and came to rest on its side at almost a right angle to the

Wreckage following the Buttevant disaster.

main line. The next two coaches also jack-knifed almost at a right angle and formed an inverted V with the preceding coach. The adjacent end of the V was hard against the goods loading bank and had struck and derailed a plough-van attached to a row of loaded ballast wagons parked against the loading bank. The rest of the train was not too severely damaged.

The most striking feature of the accident was that the damage to most vehicles was in marked contrast with the demolition of the four carriages that followed the engine and leading van. These four coaches, built between 1953 and 1964, had timber bodies and their design lacked some features that are now considered as standard in modern designs of passenger train equipment. There can be little doubt that if sufficient up-to-date carriages of integral body construction, equipped with buck-eye couplings and anti-collision gangways, had been included in the assembly of the train, the consequences of the Buttevant crash would have been less severe.

The Scene and Circumstances
Buttevant station previously served a small town of that name, but since 1977 had not been a stopping place for scheduled passenger trains on the Dublin-Cork main line. The larger stations of Charleville 13 kilometres to its north and Mallow 11 kilometres to its south catered adequately for the needs

of the small town and its surrounding countryside. A double-track railway was running through the station, which was a block post with sidings connected to both running lines used mainly by ballast trains and permanent way machines. There were platforms for both running lines and near the Charleville end of the up platform was a signal cabin controlling signals and points, as well as the adjoining gated public road level crossing.

At the time of the disaster, however, Buttevant station had an exceptional feature related to the rail development work that had been in progress in the area for several months. As may be seen from the diagrammatic plan of the station's trackwork, two trailing exits from the down siding had been removed prior to the accident and were replaced by a new facing connection to the down siding and a new crossover between the platforms to facilitate greater ease of access for the duration of the development work. Although they had been used on five or six occasions since 1 June, neither the new facing points nor the new crossover had yet been connected to the signal cabin on 1 August 1980. A crossover beyond the level crossing at the Charleville end of the station was still connected to the signal cabin, although

An aerial view of the Buttevant disaster.

it had been due for removal as part of the development work.

On the day of the disaster, train speeds were restricted to 25mph on a section of the down main line some five kilometres north of Buttevant because of track maintenance works, but there was no restriction on the general 75mph then permitted in the section that included the station itself. The weather conditions at the time of the disaster were good.

Formal Investigation

The public inquiry ordered by the Minister for Transport was conducted by Mr J. V. Feehan, Railways Inspecting Officer, in the Hibernian Hotel Mallow from 17 September to 3 October 1980. Fifty-six witnesses gave evidence under oath and the oral testimony and submissions when transcribed amounted to thirteen volumes with almost five thousand folios.

The Report of the Investigation, published in April 1981, concluded that the accident at Buttevant on 1 August 1980 occurred because a set of unconnected facing points on the down mainline were partly or wholly made into the down siding when the 10 a.m. Dublin-Cork passenger train reached them. The train travelling at about 65mph was diverted into the siding and derailed. The accident was blamed on poor communication between CIÉ staff and on inadequate safety procedures, rather than on negligence.

The report found that the procedures drawn up locally to cover the hand operation of the unconnected points and the control of movements over them were inadequate and not in compliance with the relevant CIÉ rules. In a direct criticism the report stated that 'since the facing points had been installed by the Engineering Division and were being used by that division for ballast train operations, the lapse of time in connecting them to the signal cabin was inexplicable.'

Evidence given at the investigation revealed that about thirty minutes before the accident, the facing points had been hand operated to facilitate the movement of a ballast cleaner. As the 10 a.m. Dublin-Cork passenger train approached, the points were being hand operated again by a pointsman in the mistaken belief that a recently arrived light engine from Mallow, which was standing on the up line at Buttevant near the crossover beyond the level crossing, was about to cross to the down siding. When the passenger train came into sight, the pointsman tried with a crowbar to remake the points for the main line but was unable to do so before the train reached them.

The report stressed that, for the safe regulation of railway traffic, uniform compliance with CIÉ Rules & Regulations was essential. Criticism was directed at evidence of casual supervision and a lack of that personal discipline which 'is usually found in railway personnel'. The report commented in some detail on the amount and type of damage sustained in the accident, on the number of casualties, and on the age and design of the vehicles wrecked. It concluded that the timber-bodied coaches had poor damage-resistant qualities and that the screw-shackle connections between the vehicles did not prevent them from jack-knifing. A study of similar derailment accidents abroad indicated that modern all-steel coaches mounted on heavy under-frames and fitted with buck-eye automatic couplings and Pullman gangways could survive major derailment accidents without serious damage. The report recommended that, pending the delivery of new coaches of all-steel construction, efforts should be made to ensure that all the timber-bodied coaches still in service were used only on the railway lines with light traffic and where the maximum speed did not exceed 60mph.

The report was also critical of the fact that the signalman at Buttevant had to leave his cabin for two to three minutes every time the level crossing gates had to be opened for rail traffic. At no other location on the Dublin-Cork main line was a signalman required to open and close gates in that manner. The report recommended that crossing gates that could safely be operated from inside the cabin be provided at Buttevant.

Finally, the report commented that in the circumstances obtaining at Buttevant the presence or absence of radio communication could not have affected the situation. However, in other potential or actual accident situations, the report observed that the presence of radio communication to and from trains and of voice communication between train drivers and train guards could be significant in preventing or reducing the extent of an accident, as well as improving aspects of security.

Repercussions

CIÉ accepted the thrust of the criticisms made in the report and began to revise its operating rules for the safer regulation of railway traffic. Within the restricted financial resources then at its disposal, CIÉ also began to expedite plans for replacing timber-bodied carriages with modern all-steel coaches and to introduce radio communication for better control of train movements. However, these plans were only beginning to be implemented when a further major railway accident occurred just three years later at Cherryville near Kildare.

'WE'RE OUT OF FUEL'

Seven people lost their lives and about fifty-five were injured, many of them seriously, when the 6.50 p.m. Galway-Dublin passenger ran into the rear of the stationary 5.15 p.m. Tralee-Dublin passenger train that had run out of fuel at Cherryville/*Bhaile na Siníní* near Kildare/*Cill Dara* around 9.40 p.m. on Sunday night 21 August 1983. After the crash both trains were plunged into darkness and confusion reigned as throngs of shocked passengers, mainly young people returning from a weekend in the country, made their way across a field from the wrecked trains carrying suit cases, rucksacks and guitars. Rescue workers used doors from the carriages of the Tralee train to carry the dying and seriously injured to the Kildare-Monasterevin road some 200 metres away. Scores of army personnel called out under the Kildare Emergency Plan eventually brought order to the scene and by 2 a.m. almost all of the 700 survivors, with the assistance of a large number of local volunteers, were organised into a special fleet of double-decker buses sent from Dublin. The new national pop station RTÉ Radio 2 remained on air throughout the night giving news and information about the crash.

Eyewitnesses
Most of the casualties were in the rear carriages of the stationary Tralee-Dublin train. One eyewitness said the last carriage of the Tralee train jumped 30 feet in the air with the force of the impact:

> It was unbelievable. I've seen photographs of train crashes and that's exactly what it looked like. One carriage was up in the air. It was just a tangle of metal.

A nurse travelling on the Tralee-Dublin train said they had been stopped for about fifteen minutes when there was a sudden jolt:

> We did not realize at first how bad it was. It was not possible to get some people out because they were wedged in. It seemed to take a long time for everything to come – ambulances and so on. We tried to do first aid.

The scene at Cherryville following the crash of the Galway-Dublin train into the rear of the Tralee-Dublin train on 21 August 1983.

Many passengers appeared to have broken bones. Some had broken hips. A lot of people had cuts from broken glass. But despite the shock, people were remarkably calm.

A passenger on the Galway-Dublin train, Ray Nolan of Inchicore, was travelling in the third carriage from the front of the train:

There was a big bang and a flash. All lights went out. I was thrown off my feet and the table in front of us broke into a couple of pieces.

Three teenagers returning from a holiday in Roundstone, Co Galway said there had been a lot of stoppages along the line before the train crashed:

Our train was going dead slow. There were red lights along the way. It was misty outside. Suddenly there was a bang. We were a few carriages down and didn't feel it too badly, but some people were a bit shook.

It was only when we got out that we saw the front of the train up in the air and carriages thrown all over the place, all squashed up. There were a lot of people with broken shoulders and cuts from broken glass. People were screaming and a priest was going around giving the last sacraments to some of the injured who were lying beside the train.

A local man who arrived on the scene an hour after the crash and helped pull some of the injured free said some people were crying and distressed, but most remained calm. Reporters arriving later said this was borne out by the demeanour of those who were walking uninjured along the country roads.

The Trains Involved

On leaving Tralee the 5.15 p.m. train to Dublin consisted of ten vehicles hauled by 071 class engine No 079. However, this engine broke down in Millstreet, Co Cork and when restarted managed to reach Mallow about 20 minutes late. There a replacement locomotive was requested by the driver and he was given an A class engine No 009 that had recently arrived from Waterford. The fuel tank of the replacement engine was not checked by the driver, as he assumed it had been full leaving Waterford and would have adequate fuel to get to Dublin. The train continued its journey to Dublin, but was now 31 minutes late. By the time it left Thurles, there were 337 passengers on board. After passing through Monasterevin station in Co Kildare, the driver noticed that the tone of the locomotive's engine changed. Soon after, the engine cut out and the train coasted to a stop just short of Cherryville Junction, where a single-track line from Kilkenny and Waterford joins the double-track Dublin-Cork main line.

The driver got out and began walking down the track to consult with the guard, whom he met six or seven carriages back from the locomotive. He told the guard 'We're out of fuel.'

It was agreed that the driver would walk ahead to the next signal to telephone for assistance, while the guard would protect the train in the rear in accordance with Rule 188 that requires detonators to be placed on the track at a quarter mile, half mile and one mile behind a stationary train. The driver had not gone far ahead of his engine when he heard a locomotive approaching from the rear and then saw its searchlight and heard a bang. As he was aware that a train from Dublin was due shortly on the down line, he placed detonators on that line for about a mile before he attempted to make contact with the signalman at Centralised Traffic Control (CTC) in Connolly Station, Dublin. Unfortunately, his attempts were frustrated by defective and malfunctioning telephones.

Meanwhile the guard had collected his detonators from the van at the rear of his train, checked that the tail lamp was lighting and was about to set off down the track when he saw the headlight of an approaching locomotive. He thought it might be coming to give assistance by pushing his train in the rear and he put down two detonators about 100 metres from his stationary train. But the approaching locomotive and the first two carriages had just passed him when the crash happened.

The 6.50 p.m. train from Galway, headed by 071 class engine No 086 and hauling eight vehicles, was running on schedule and had 374 passengers on board when it reached Portarlington. Here the Galway train joined the Dublin-Cork main line for the last leg of its journey to Dublin. According to the evidence of the train's guard, the train ran normally after Portarlington for about eight kilometres until it was stopped by a red signal indicating danger. The train waited for nine minutes at the red signal while the driver unsuccessfully tried to contact the signalman at CTC in Connolly Station Dublin by lineside telephone. Then the locomotive hooted and the train moved off at about 25mph according to the guard. The next signal was displaying a yellow aspect, signifying the need for caution, but the train's speed did not change. Very shortly afterwards the crash happened. Immediately after the impact, the guard checked that the driver was all right and asked him to protect the down line with detonators, while he walked back to protect his train in the rear.

Formal Investigation

Within five days of the accident, the Minister for Transport, Jim Mitchell TD, ordered that a formal investigation be conducted into its causes and circumstances by the Railways Inspecting Officer, Mr J. V. Feehan. The investigation opened in the City Hall, Dublin on 19 September 1983 and continued until 23 September, when it was adjourned pending the outcome of court proceedings against the driver of one of the trains involved in the accident. The investigation was resumed in the City Hall on 8 June 1984 and continued until 20 June. A total of 48 witnesses gave evidence under oath.

The Report of the Investigation, published in December 1984, found that the accident on 21 August 1983 occurred because the 6.50 p.m. Galway-Dublin passenger train proceeded past an automatic stop signal at danger, when the driver could not contact the signalman by telephone or by radio. The train was running at such speed that allowing for visibility, condition of the rails and gradients of the line, the driver, when he became aware of an obstruction on the line ahead, could not stop his train before it collided with the 5.15 p.m. Tralee-Dublin passenger train which was stationary. The signal post telephone (SPT) at the danger signal and the radio in the locomotive of the Galway-Dublin train were both unserviceable.

The Investigating Officer observed that CIÉ Rule 55 permitted a driver to proceed cautiously past an automatic stop signal without authorisation from the controlling signalman when the SPT was unserviceable. Rule 55, however, did not specify a maximum speed at which a train might proceed cautiously where the reason for a stop signal being at danger was unknown. The officer noted that a petition signed by fifty drivers and handed in during the investigation stated that there was unease at the absence of any interpretation of how trains should proceed cautiously.

Wrecked carriages at Cherryville after the August 1983 crash.

The officer recommended that in no circumstances should a train proceed past any stop signal at danger without prior permission from the controlling signalman. When such permission was given, the train should proceed cautiously only as far as the line is seen to be clear, at a speed of not more than 10mph in conditions of good visibility in daylight and at a considerably lower speed during periods of reduced visibility and during the hours of darkness.

The Investigating Officer pointed out that if either the locomotive radio on the Galway-Dublin train or the SPT had been serviceable the accident might have been avoided. He was very critical of the number of faults reported annually in SPTs. This 'fell short of the standards to be expected in a modern railway communication system'. He recommended improvement in the reliability of the SPT system and its retention in operational service for at least two years after the new planned discrete train radio system came into full operational use and its reliability had been proven.

As in the report of the investigation into the 1980 Buttevant accident, the report on the Cherryville accident stressed that uniform interpretation and strict implementation of rules, signalling regulations and instructions are essential requirements for the safe and orderly running of trains. The report was very critical that, notwithstanding the Buttevant report, the two trains involved in the accident at Cherryville included between them a total of six timber-bodied carriages, including the buffet car on the Tralee-Dublin train that was completely destroyed.

A guard-to-driver voice conversation system for all trains with guards aboard was also recommended in the report, as well as the replacement of oil tail lamps by two large electric tail lamps that should be lighting at all times when trains are in service. Finally, improved procedures for recording the fueling of locomotives both for scheduled and unscheduled duties was recommended to avoid any future incident of a train engine running out of fuel. It emerged at the inquiry that the replacement engine No 009 provided at Mallow for the Tralee train had undertaken an earlier unscheduled run from Waterford to Arklow and return before its scheduled duty to Mallow. That unscheduled run had not been recorded, thus causing No 009 to have insufficient fuel to complete the final 50 kilometres of its journey to Dublin on that tragic August night in 1983.

PART FOUR

BOMBINGS, ROBBERIES AND A DERAILMENT

SABOTAGE AT MEIGH

Following the emergence of a powerful civil rights movement in Northern Ireland in 1969 a state of near-revolutionary crisis developed that has been generally referred to as 'The Troubles'. The vehemence with which reform in Northern Ireland was being resisted led to the placing of the British army on the streets in August of that year. Faced with increasing civil strife, the local Stormont government in August 1971 introduced internment without trial with disastrous results. A sharp upsurge in violence ensued and following the killing of thirteen civilians by the British army in Derry and the consequent burning of the British embassy in Dublin in January 1972, the Stormont parliament collapsed. The British government then had little choice but to impose direct rule from London in March 1972. Violence escalated widely during the following years and those imprisoned in the internment camps, which continued to be used until December 1975, were themselves radicalised by the experience. The convulsed situation in Northern Ireland contributed in no small way to the numerous acts of sabotage unleashed against the railways throughout Ireland during the 1970s.

One of the first major acts of sabotage took place at Meigh, Co Armagh in August 1973. At that time Meigh/*Maigh* boasted a small signalbox on the double-track Dublin-Belfast main line guarding a level crossing in a rural area of South Armagh, some 15 kilometres north of Dundalk and just a short distance within the border of Northern Ireland. On the night of 15 August 1973 a gang of ten men, some of them armed, ordered the signalman to stop the 10.15 p.m. Derry goods train approaching from Dundalk. This train was hauled by Bo-Bo diesel electric engine No B201 and included a van of mails and a dozen wagons with containers. The raiders ordered the signalman, the driver and guard to depart. They obeyed and headed for the village of Meigh over a kilometre to the west to raise the alarm. The raiding gang then placed two milk-cans containing a heavy charge of explosives at the locomotive, the engine of which was still running, and robbed the mailbags from the van before making off.

Meigh crossing in 1997, re-built and re-opened as an automatic barrier crossing after 23 years of violence.

When a detachment of British troops arrived, it was decided it would be too dangerous to approach the train, as its engine was still 'ticking over' and using up fuel. By midday on 16 August a decision was reached to try and see what could be achieved with accurate shooting. An army marksman was engaged to focus on the connection between the milk-cans and the engine. With his ninth shot, he cut the connection between the two cans, but caused an instant flash that was followed by a loud explosion. When the smoke cleared, the locomotive was no more. Only the large diesel engine was left above the twisted remains of the wheel-bogies and frame, with some semblance of a cab at one end. Some damage was also caused to the track, but emergency repairs enabled single-line working to be restored later that same evening. The remains of engine No B201 were hauled away to Dundalk and later removed to Inchicore Works in Dublin, where a decision was later reached to scrap the ill-fated locomotive.

Within two months of this first major act of sabotage, a second serious incident took place at the exact same location. On 23 October 1973 the 2.15 a.m. Belfast goods train coming from Dundalk was similarly 'hijacked' near Meigh. The train was hauled by A-class diesel electric engine No 008 and included eleven cement hoppers and a dozen wagons with some containers. On this occasion bombs were planted in the engine and when the British troops were given the alarm they were reluctant to approach the train in fear that it might have been booby-trapped.

Their apprehension was reinforced later that day when at 1 p.m. a group of journalists narrowly escaped an explosion that was triggered off in a ditch near where they were standing. Later that afternoon there was a violent explosion within the locomotive and it damaged engine No 008 beyond repair. However, only the engine was destroyed and the goods train emerged unscathed. The following day the remains of engine No 008 were towed to Dundalk and by the afternoon of 24 October 1973 the line had been cleared to allow the resumption of some of the services on the Dublin-Belfast main line.

Despite the remarkable efficiency with which the main line was restored to traffic after these serious incidents, considerable disruption was caused to the Dublin-Belfast services by numerous bomb threats and other incidents during the 1970s. Shortly after the serious incidents related above, the engine drivers based in Dundalk came to a decision to refuse to operate trains over the Border between 9.30 p.m. and 7.00 a.m. and alternative arrangements had to be made for the transfer of mails by road at night.

The action of the drivers gathered increasing support as the number and frequency of incidents multiplied. On 27 October a bomb scare at Poyntzpass caused the cancellation of both the 6.25 a.m. Mail to Portadown and the 8.30 a.m. Dublin-Belfast train beyond Dundalk. Within a week, on 1 November, the signalman at Poyntzpass was forced from his cabin at gunpoint, but later resumed duty under military guard, and that night a hijacked lorry was placed across the main line at Meigh. Two days later a train ran through another lorry at the same spot. As this lorry was suspected of having bombs in it, the Dublin-Belfast mainline remained closed for an entire weekend causing disruption, confusion and great anxiety among the brave travelling public.

Many people during those troubled years wondered what contribution, apart from creating chaos, could possibly have been made towards achieving political and social reform in Northern Ireland by these continual rail disruptions. What many commentators overlooked was the fact that goods trains were primarily targeted and that passenger trains largely escaped damage in the border area. The reason for this concentration of attack on freight movements by rail was to remove the option of rail transport for goods traffic, thereby forcing all goods movements into and out of Northern Ireland to go by road. In conditions where lorry drivers crossing the Border at their peril had to pay 'protection money' in order to continue working, it was no wonder that sending goods by rail had to be strongly discouraged by those seeking to profit from those lawless times!

ROBBERY AT DUNDALK

On 20 February 1973, during the escalation of violence on the railways in Ireland, an armed gang of seven men and a woman held up the 8 a.m. Dublin-Belfast *Enterprise*, together with its passengers, the station staff and Customs staff, as it pulled into Dundalk/*Dún Dealgan* station. Eight mailbags were taken from the train and the gang escaped across the tracks to a nearby roadway where stolen cars and accomplices were waiting for them. The value of the goods taken was of the order of £50,000. By coincidence, this high-profile robbery took place during the second week of a national CIÉ low fares promotion campaign being widely advertised in the national media as the 'Great Train Robbery' – a fact that gave rise to many facetious remarks at the expense of CIÉ.

Looking north from the main platform of Dundalk station where the robbery of the Dublin-Belfast train took place on 20 February 1973.

THE RUNAWAY TO PORTADOWN

A highly dangerous and irresponsible runaway incident was deliberately created by an armed group when they hijacked the 3.30 a.m. Dublin-Belfast newspaper train early in the morning of 8 November 1974. The short train consisted only of re-engined A-class locomotive No A60R hauling a single bogie van loaded with Dublin newspapers for distribution in the North. The train was stopped at the former station of Mount Pleasant in Co Louth, just short of the border with Northern Ireland. The crew was ordered off at gunpoint and the engine was then sent northwards at full throttle. The driverless train travelled unimpeded for over 48 kilometres until it reached the approach to Portadown/*Port an Dúnain* station. There the speeding train failed to take the sharp curve into the station and both the locomotive and van were derailed, totally blocking the double-track main line.

Runaway engine No A60R, after it failed to take the sharp curve into Portadown station on 9 November 1974.

An anonymous phone call claimed that there were explosives on board and, while this was being checked out, a number of nearby houses were evacuated. No explosives were found and local rail services to Belfast could operate again by 8.30 a.m. One of the main lines was cleared the same evening allowing Dublin-Belfast services to resume, but A60R was not recovered until five days later when the CIÉ steam crane from Inchicore in Dublin managed to re-rail the damaged locomotive on 13 November. The bogie newspaper van, however, was so badly damaged in the derailment that it was decided to cut it up for scrap at the accident site.

Wrecked engine A 60R at Portadown. Note the CIE steam crane from Inchicore at the extreme right.

SCARE AT SCARVA

A serious incident that could have caused much loss of life occurred near Scarva/*Scarbhach* station in Co Down on 6 February 1976 when a device exploded on the outer rail under the 5.30 p.m. Belfast-Dublin CIÉ *Enterprise* train. This was the most serious attack on a passenger train during the Troubles and caused engine B174 and all six carriages of the train to be derailed. It was most fortunate that at the time of the incident a speed restriction of 30mph was in force on that section of track at Anderson's Bridge just north of Scarva where the malicious explosion took place.

The fact that the train was exclusively made up of modern all-steel carriages with buck-eye couplings was a significant factor in preventing the train from disintegrating on derailment. Another fortunate factor was the site, because the derailed train came to rest leaning on the bank of a cutting. Had the explosion occurred 100 metres nearer to Belfast the derailed carriages would probably have ploughed into the abutment of an overbridge. If the bomb had been placed on the inner side of the track, the vehicles would have turned on their sides across the other track and probably would have led to more considerable damage and casualties.

In the event only four people had to be brought to hospital and damage to the track was relatively light. Most of the 200 passengers on this CIÉ train were brought to a local hall, where local residents kindly provided them with tea and refreshments. Afterwards they were brought to nearby Scarva station, from where the uninjured passengers continued their journey south by a special NIR train.

The Belfast-Dublin *Enterprise* after its derailment by explosion near Scarva on 6 February 1976.

GUNFIRE AT WICKLOW

During the wave of anger and unrest that spread from Northern Ireland during the 1970s, several instances of serious raids and robberies occurred throughout Ireland not only on banks and property but also affecting the railways. Some were particularly serious and had significant political repercussions.

Early on 12 March 1976 at about 4.45 a.m. the signalman at Wicklow was unloading a mail van of the 3.25 a.m. Dublin-Wexford newspaper train when an armed gang of six men approached and directed their attention on another van in the train. Apparently that particular van contained a substantial sum in banknotes destined for banks and post offices throughout the south-east. Because of the increasing incidents of raids on trains, the van also carried armed members of the Special Branch of the Garda Síochána. The raiders, apparently unaware of their presence, began to open the van when they were greeted with gunfire. In a panic, they immediately fled making their getaway across adjoining fields to avoid capture by the local gardaí.

The Special Branch detectives, using walkie-talkie appartatus, then instructed the driver to pull his train out of the station and, in the confusion, the signalman jumped into the nearest bogie van and stayed with the moving train, while holding the train staff needed for the Wicklow-Greystones section. It happened that the 10.30 p.m. night goods train from Wexford was crossing the newspaper train at Wicklow, but it could not now depart for Greystones without the obligatory train staff. The detectives then became extremely suspicious that the Dublin-bound goods train was not immediately departing and asked that it should be fully examined in search of the missing armed raiders. But none was found, as they had long since vanished into the night.

THE SALLINS MAIL TRAIN ROBBERY

Following the attempted robbery of substantial cash funds at Wicklow station on 12 March 1976, it was decided to strengthen security arrangements for the transfer of money by rail. Notwithstanding that decision, a much more serious incident took place less than three weeks later involving a train that had no armed security personnel on board.

The 9.20 p.m. Night Mail left Cork for Dublin on 30 March 1976 with a substantial amount of unguarded cash in mailbags and parcels. Somehow, the fact that the train's contents were not under armed surveillance became known to one of those gangs seeking to fund their activities with substantial sums of money. This extraordinary leakage of information was not only most embarrassing to all directly involved in the transportation arrangements, but it also had very serious political implications for successive governments over a period of almost twenty years.

As the Cork-Dublin Night Mail was approaching Hazelhatch in Co Kildare shortly before 3.00 a.m. on 31 March 1976, the driver heard a series of detonators exploding on the track beneath the engine and quickly brought his train to a halt expecting some emergency ahead. A man wearing a CIÉ permanent way worker's suit approached along the track carrying a red lamp. When he reached the head of the train and climbed up into the driver's cab, he produced a gun and ordered the driver to reverse his train a distance of about three kilometres to milepost 11.75. There a number of raiders climbed up from the tracks and with military precision they entered the train, going directly to the vans containing the mailbags and the parcels of money. When all the relevant items had been selected, the bags and parcels were thrown down to a number of waiting cars that drove off as soon as they were loaded. The entire operation was conducted most efficiently in military style and was completed within ten minutes. Central Traffic Control at Connolly Station Dublin had noted the train's delay of ten minutes in the Sallins-Hazelhatch section and, becoming suspicious, notified the gardaí. But by the time they reached the relatively remote location of the robbery near Sallins/ *Na Solláin*, the raiders had long since made their escape.

When the train was examined it was discovered that almost a quarter of a million pounds had been stolen, causing public consternation and great annoyance at government level. Extreme pressure was exerted on the Garda Síochána to apprehend those responsible without delay. Huge round-ups of suspects took place, resulting in several dozen arrests. In later legal proceedings it was said that unacceptable levels of physical and psychological torture had been used by the Special Branch of the Garda Síochána to extract confessions of guilt from innocent young men. Six members of the Irish Republican Socialist Party were originally charged with the mail train robbery, but the charges against them were dismissed. Four were then re-charged and sent for trial at the Special Criminal Court, but only three were found guilty. They were sent to jail, amid cries of there being a miscarriage of justice based on confessions extracted by alleged police brutality. Public unease was not allayed when one of those found guilty, Nicky Kelly of Arklow, absconded while on bail. As the other two found guilty were subsequently freed by the Court of Criminal Appeal, Nicky Kelly believing himself to be safe returned from the US only to be re-arrested and jailed for four years before being released in 1984.

The political repercussions for the government did not end there. Nicky Kelly and his colleagues, enraged by the way they had been made scape-goats for successive governments embarrassed by the Sallins mail train robbery in 1976, decided to pursue the state for damages to the highest level in the courts. The members of the Irish Republican Socialist Party were fully vindicated when the Supreme Court finally ruled in 1995 that they had been wronged and awarded damages against the state amounting to three-quarters of a million pounds. Between that award and the amount stolen from the train almost twenty years earlier, over one million pounds was lost because of the mishandling of the aftermath of the Sallins Mail train robbery.

HUGE EXPLOSION

O ne of the largest railway explosions in the recent Troubles took place on 21 April 1979 when a special goods train from Dundalk to Belfast was hijacked around 8 a.m. at Kilnasagart Bridge near the Border between the Republic and Northern Ireland. Two milk-churns packed with explosives were loaded into the rear cab of the A-class diesel locomotive No 046. The crew was then forced at gunpoint to take the train some seven kilometres further north and to stop at Killeen Bridge/ *Droichead Chillín* under the main Dublin-Belfast road, thus effectively blocking both main rail and road arteries. Some lorries were also placed on the road, but these were later found to contain no explosives.

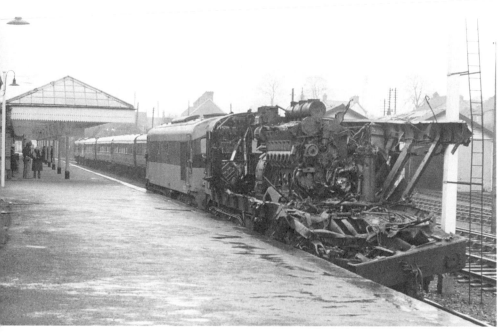

Wreckage of engine No 046 seen at Dundalk, having been towed from Killeen Bridge on 22 April 1979.

Shortly afterwards, when the crew had left the train, an extremely large explosion took place wrecking No 046 and badly damaging an empty container and two bogie fertilizer wagons. That evening the train was carefully examined by British army experts and declared free of further explosives. On the following morning 22 April work began on clearing away the wreckage. It was first believed that the high overbridge was severely damaged but after detailed examination it was declared safe. Then with much trouble the remains of the heavy locomotive were removed south to Dundalk, where the accompanying photograph was taken. By 3.30 p.m. that day, the main line had been cleared and the regular 6 p.m. up and down *Enterprise* express trains resumed operation. The crippled engine No 046 was removed on 25 April from Dundalk to Inchicore Works in Dublin where it was subsequently cut up for scrap.

DRIVERLESS TO GORAGHWOOD

Towards the end of the period of frequent attacks against the railways in the 1970s, a most dangerous act of sabotage took place that ended at Goraghwood/*Coill an Ghoraigh* near Newry, Co Down. On 23 July 1979 an early morning northbound goods train on the Dublin-Belfast line was stopped by armed men south of the Border near Mountpleasant, Co Louth. The crew was ordered out and forced at gunpoint to isolate the safety control equipment on the A class diesel engine No 004. The freight train was then sent driverless over the Border and down the long incline towards Newry, Co Down. Eventually the train derailed itself at Goraghwood, the site of the former junction with the branch line to Newry and Warrenpoint, having travelled a total distance of over 20 kilometres from Mountpleasant. On derailment the engine slid some distance on its side, caught fire and was

Goraghwood station with a train entering from Newry. The line from Dublin is on the right.

extensively damaged. The train was a short one and the wagons were telescoped and overturned clear of the track. Miraculously nobody was injured in this outrageous incident. The line was quickly cleared and single-line working was restored in time for that afternoon's *Enterprise* express trains.

THE SPECTACULAR DUNLEER ROBBERY

An armed gang of eight men staged a most spectacular train robbery on 12 July 1999 at the closed station of Dunleer/*Dún Léire* in Co Louth on the Dubiln-Belfast main line. Using a heavy crane, they removed a 12 metre container of cigarettes valued at €925,000 en route from Carroll's Factory in Dundalk to Dublin Port from a passing goods train in the full light of day in what must have been one of the most daring train robberies ever committed in Ireland.

Under bogus pretences, the paramilitary gang hired a heavy crane to go to a work site at Drogheda bus station. When it arrived there they put a gun to the driver's head and forced him to drive the crane some 16 kilometres north of Drogheda to the closed and secluded station of Dunleer. Meanwhile other members of the gang already arrived at the station had kidnapped the permanent way track-walker who was responsible for checking the safety of the tracks on a daily basis. They confiscated the detonators he held to warn trains of unexpected damage or obstruction on the running lines and then placed the detonators along the up line track towards Belfast. Within a short time their work had the desired effect. The 2 p.m. Dundalk-North Wall goods train approached hauled by engine No 081 and as soon as the detonators began to explode, the train driver applied his brakes and pulled to a stop at the platform of the closed station at Dunleer.

No time was lost by the gang in completing their planned robbery. With scant regard for the safety of any train that might be travelling on the down line track from Dublin, they used their crane to lift the 12 metre container from the halted goods train on the up line across the down line and on to a waiting lorry and trailer parked on the down platform. Immediately the lorry drove off with its valuable cargo. Then one of the armed gang shepherded the track-walker, the crane-driver and the security man on to the goods train and forced its crew at gunpoint to drive it south for a distance of 56 kilometres to Portmarnock station in Co Dublin. At this quiet station all the captives were tied up by the gang, who then made their getaway in a waiting car.

EPILOGUE

THE BIG SCARE OF KNOCKCROGHERY

On Saturday, 8 November 1997 an ominous and frightening accident occurred near Knockcroghery/*Cnoc an Chrochaire* in Co Roscommon when every single vehicle of the 8.25 a.m. Dublin-Westport passenger train became derailed because of the poor condition of the track. Fortunately the train was lightly loaded with only 156 passengers on board and there were no serious injuries to either passengers or crew. What undoubtedly contributed to the absence of serious injury was the train's good fortune in derailing within a shallow cutting, the sides of which prevented the carriages from toppling over. It was an accident just waiting to happen and could so easily have become a major disaster. The fact that it was caused by unstable and unsafe track set off alarm bells at all levels of responsibility from the government down to those charged with daily management of the railways in Ireland.

The train involved, headed by 201 class engine No 211 hauling seven modern coaches, was derailed at Curry level crossing in the Knockcroghery-Roscommon section of the Mayo line. The locomotive remained on the rails, but the first three vehicles were partly derailed and the other four badly derailed. Approximately 440 metres of track were damaged in the derailment and in consequence the line was closed until the evening of 10 November to allow two large road cranes lift the derailed coaches back on to the rails.

Public Disquiet

The accident caused serious public disquiet, not least because its location was in the native county of the then Minister for Public Enterprise, Mary O'Rourke TD, who was politically responsible for CIÉ. Public concern was expressed about the safety of rail travel, particularly in the light of government policy over the previous decade to invest vast capital sums in roads and only allocate minimal funds to the railways. When additional speed restrictions were introduced on most lines – apart from the Dublin-Belfast and Dublin-Cork main lines – following the Knockcroghery derailment, many people chose to travel by faster road services rather than by the slower and less

The derailed train at Knockcroghery, Co Roscommon on 8 November 1997.

dependable trains. Iarnród Éireann (IÉ) continually apologised for train delays due to speed restrictions and explained that its railway network had been deprived of significant capital investment for over a decade.

In this crisis situation, the Department of Public Enterprise consulted urgently with IÉ and with its parent body CIÉ before the question of rail safety was brought urgently to the government's attention by the Minister for Public Enterprise early in December. To help allay public disquiet, the minister subsequently announced the government's intention to establish a strategic review by independent consultants into all aspects of rail safety. The review would centre on the adequacy of IÉ's safety policy, systems, rules and procedures, and would cover aspects such as trackwork, signalling, rolling stock and level crossings. The contract for the Rail Safety Study was awarded early in 1998 to an international consortium headed by International Risk Management Services (IRMS) of Cheshire, United Kingdom.

Safety Studies

Meanwhile the inquiry conducted by IÉ into the derailment found that it occurred on a section of jointed track two miles west of Knockcroghery and that its direct cause had been the failure of a track joint, which in turn had been brought about by the weakening of the trackbed beneath the joint. This led to the breakage of two fishplates under the action of passing trains. Since the derailment, IÉ had taken a number of initiatives to improve operational safety on the railway, including the strengthening of the inspection process for jointed track and a review of train operating speeds with some additional restrictions being introduced. In presenting the inquiry report to the Minister for Public Enterprise on 6 February 1998, IÉ noted that international experts were being engaged to review maintenance procedures and make recommendations on the priorities to be followed in the replacement of jointed track with continuous welded rail (CWR).

The IRMS report on the Rail Safety Study was presented to the government on 9 November 1998. The report noted that, historically, the Irish railway system had been safe with the level of reportable accidents and casualties comparable with other European networks. However, the shortfall of investment in the railways in recent years was impacting on safety, while the reliance IÉ was placing on the experience and skill of individual staff was being undermined as many of the older generation were leaving the service. The IMRS report considered that the condition of the railway infrastructure was unacceptable in many areas. The condition of track, signalling and structures was found to be generally poor, whereas rolling stock was considered satisfactory. The risk analysis model developed by the consultants predicted that there was a potential risk of ten accidents, which could result in about seven fatalities a year in the short-term, if no improvements were made. The IMRS report estimated that about £590million would need to be spent over the following 15 years to bring the IÉ railway system up to the required international safety standards. As an immediate response to the IRMS report, the government authorised CIÉ to borrow £23million towards the initial cost of addressing safety issues.

In addition to the IRMS safety report sought by the Minister for Public Enterprise, the Board of CIÉ commissioned the consultancy firm Arthur D. Little Ltd (ADL) to conduct an independent safety review of rail infrastructure on its behalf. Their report was very critical of the rundown state of much of the railway network. They found that many of the rails were overage and badly worn, many of the wooden sleepers were decaying, many lengths of track were beyond economical repair and patch re-sleepering, while vital for safe day-to-day operation, was expensive and provided little long-term value in reducing failures. ADL recommended that a rolling programme of 120 kilometres of track renewals each year over five years be urgently put in place to allow the continued safe operation of passenger rail services. Interestingly, the Mullingar-Sligo line and the Athlone-Westport line, on which the Knockcroghery derailment happened, were identified as the two lines needing the most urgent attention. A rolling programme of signalling renewals was also recommended, as well as a robust and positive regime of signalling maintenance to prevent further neglect and deterioration of equipment, especially at Heuston Station Dublin and at Limerick – both being strategic locations.

Rail Safety Programme
In the light of the recommendations of both the IRMS and the ADL reports on rail safety, the Minister for Public Enterprise Mary O'Rourke TD announced early in 1999 the government's approval for the implementation on a £430million Rail Safety Programme for the five-year period 1999-2003. The programme provided mainly for track renewals, but also for signalling and telecommunications, structures and fencing, level crossings, rolling stock and safety management systems. The Minister also made an important and significant announcement that there was now a government commitment to the retention of all the rail network then existing, bringing to an end the long period of uncertainty about the future of the railways created by the lack of any significant investment since the mid-1980s.

Since 1999 the railways in Ireland have been transformed. In addition to the Dublin-Belfast and Dublin-Cork double-track main lines, the other single-track inter-city lines from Dublin to Sligo, Westport, Galway, Limerick, Tralee, Waterford and Rosslare Europort have been virtually rebuilt with CWR on concrete sleepers, computerised automatic signaling, centralised traffic control, reinforced embankments, automatic level crossings, modernised terminal stations and all-steel coaches with buck-eye couplings and anti-collision connecting gangways.

Today's modern Irish railway system is unrecognisable from that which was struggling along only ten years ago. Considering that new regular-interval accelerated train services with the most modern inter-city fleet of coaches in Europe is to be introduced in stages by IÉ from 2006 to 2008, bringing even higher standards of safety and reliability to our rail transport network, it can truly be said that the big scare of the Knockcroghery derailment in 1997 provided the necessary wake-up call that has secured for Ireland in the twenty-first century a railway system with minimal risks of any further major accidents.

APPENDICES

1

RECOVERING NO 18 FROM
THE RIVER SLANEY

The task of recovering this powerful locomotive from the muddy bottom of the River Slaney was formidable. Only for two hours at low tide could the gang work at the engine and then in deep mud. Their first job was to get the engine on its wheels. To do that a solid platform had to be provided from which lifting jacks could be operated. This the breakdown gang contrived in the form of a crib of sleepers built out in the river. To build the crib, they compacted the sleepers into two-layer rafts, each layer at right angles to the other and each sleeper spiked to every one below. The sleepers were 13 centimetres thick of memel pine and reasonably easy to drill. The mud was to a depth of four rafts which they sank by levering them down with long beams, using the engine as fulcrum and putting pressure on each corner of the raft in turn, round and round, until they had it lying solid on the bottom.

From the crib they jacked up the engine to an angle of 45 degrees. Then they inserted a pitch-pine baulk across between the frame and the boiler and, by jacking up the outer end of it, tipped the engine over on to its wheels. The engine now stood with its large 1.5 metre driving wheels over their axles in mud. The next job was to get rails under the engine. That meant lifting it in one piece clear of the mud. For that task they sank two more raft-cribs, fore and aft of the engine, from which they jacked it up. Then, underneath the engine, they sank other rafts and on them laid rails under the wheels. After that, rails were laid ahead of No 18 on a succession of rafts for some 50 metres until the gang got the engine out on to the firm strand.

'From there,' said Inspector Forde, 'we were making the road as we went.' A line was laid along the shore for some 200 metres to the Slaney Bridge and up the ramp on to its causeway. The gang moved the wrecked engine up a ten-metre embankment by means of the breakdown engine hauling at the end of a 500 metre tow-rope. This rope was made ' by shackling together all the anchor chains that could be borrowed along the Quay of Wexford and more brought from Dublin'. Inspector Forde admitted 'It was a long job and in the course of it they even used the extra services of many a passing engine as long as she could be spared from her train'.

Arrived at the causeway of the bridge, the gang had to tow the engine through a right angle to face it along the county road. To this end, they laid the rails on boiler-plates to act as skids, on which they slewed the engine round with jacks. When they had room to manoeuvre, they completed the turning by working the engine back and forth on a short length of rail, slewing round the tail end it was not at that moment sitting on. So the gang faced No 18 towards the railway embankment and levered the engine through the embankment bridge with bars. At the far end, the gang turned the engine again parallel with the embankment to face up the hill of the station road, where the breakdown engine once more took No 18 in tow. At station level, they ran the engine on to the loading bank of the goods yard and left it there for some time. Getting No 18 back to the running rails was another day's work. The sleeper-rafts were left in the River Slaney where they were, as it would have cost more to salvage them than they were worth.

2

LETTER TO D&SER IN PRAISE OF
INSPECTOR MICHAEL FORDE

(White's Hotel, Wexford, October 22, 1923)

Sir,

On behalf of the Commercial Travellers, Business Men and Traders of the County Wexford and surrounding districts, we respectfully wish to call to your notice our great appreciation of the services rendered to the whole of the business community by Mr Michael Forde, Permanent Way Inspector of your Company.

For the past two years the businessmen of Ireland have managed to carry on their work with the greatest difficulty. And in this County we were faced with greater obstacles than in any other. For nearly the whole period of the recent strifes, the Co. Wexford was subjected to an almost perpetual warfare, and the Railway was nearly always the object of attack.

We were entirely dependent for the purpose of our business on the running of goods and passenger trains, and only while these were satisfactorily maintained could we hope to get our work done. In spite of every difficulty your Company gallantly managed to continue the services, and we believe that this was mainly achieved by the splendid efforts of your Permanent Way Inspector. It has come to our knowledge that Mr Forde carried out his duties during all this time at grave personal risk and that he even had to work at times under actual fire; and that, were it not for his courage, energy and self-sacrifice, the business life of the Co. Wexford would have come to a stand-still which would have meant ruin and disaster to a great number of us.

The heartfelt thanks of the whole community are due to the Company for the way it maintained the service; and we cannot too well express our appreciation of the splendid work done by Mr Forde.

We remain, yours faithfully,

(Here follow forty signatures)

3

RAILROAD PROTECTION CORPS
ARMOURED TRAINS 1922-23

Train No	Base	Operations Composition
No 1	Clonmel	One armoured locomotive, one partially-armoured box-wagon and two flat wagons.
No 2	Thurles	One armoured locomotive, two fully-armoured cars, one box-wagon and two flat wagons.
No 3	Limerick	One armoured locomotive, two fully-armoured cars and two flat wagons.
No 4	Cork	One armoured locomotive, two fully-armoured cars, one partially-armoured box-wagon and two flat wagons.
No 5	Cork	One armoured locomotive, one fully-armoured wagon and one flat wagon.
No 6	Cork	One armoured locomotive, one fully-armoured car and one flat wagon.
No 7	Dublin	One armoured locomotive and two fully-armoured cars.
No 8	Dundalk	One partially-armoured locomotive and two fully-armoured cars.

No 9   Mullingar   One armoured locomotive, two fully-armoured
                              cars and an additional separate armoured
                              locomotive, named *King Tutankhamun.*

Source: *The Irish Civil War 1922-1923: A Military Study* by Paul V Walsh.
(Paper delivered to NYMAS, New York, on 11 December 1998.)

2-4-2T engine No 64 of the D&SER forming part of an armoured train at Grand
Canal Dock, Dublin in April 1923, prior to its being sent to Cork to confront anti-
Treaty forces.

SIGNIFICANT IRISH RAILWAY ACCIDENTS SINCE 1853

Date	Location	Casualties		Comments
		Killed	Injured	
8 Oct 1853	Straffan, Co Kildare	15	8	Goods train crashed into rear of Cork-Dublin train at station.
29 Oct 1864	Ballinasloe, Co Galway	2	34	Excess speed on poor track.
9 Aug 1867	Bray Head, Co Wicklow	2	23	Derailed train fell into ravine.
13 May 1871	Ballymacarrett, Co Down	2	50	Train crashed into derailed locomotive.
30 June 1886	Brackagh Moss, Co Armagh	6	29	Derailed on defective track.
12 June 1889	Killuney, Co Armagh	88	260	Crowded runaway carriages crashed into following train.
21 June 1891	Springtown, Co Derry	2	14	Troop Special crashed head-on into empty train.
22 May 1893	Camp, Co Kerry	3	13	Pig Special crashed over viaduct at speed.
14 Feb 1900	Harcourt Street, Dublin	–	1	Cattle Special crashed through end-wall of station.

Brackagh Moss derailment south of Portadown on 30 June 1886 that resulted in six being killed and 29 injured.

11 April 1903	Frenchlawn, Co Roscommon	1	15	Mayo Night Mail crashed into an obstruction on the line.
5 Aug 1912	Lombardstown, Co Cork	1	99	Killarney tourist train derailed.
24 June 1921	Adavoyle, Co Armagh	6	–	Troop Special of 10th Huzzars mined and all horses killed.
19 Jan 1923	Ardfert, Co Kerry	2	–	Sabotage of track causing train to fall down embankment.
30 Jan 1925	Owencarrow, Co Donegal	4	4	Coaches blown off viaduct in gale.
22 Dec 1944	Straboe, Co Laois	1	–	Night Mail crashed into cattle train stalled by lack of steam and poor fuel.
10 Jan 1945	Victoria Park, Co Down	23	41	Motor train crashed into rear of crowded commuter train in fog.

14 Dec 1945	Donabate, Co Dublin	2	1	Engine firebox perforated by broken connecting rod.
6 Sept 1946	Gortavoy, Co Tyrone	1	–	Culvert collapse caused goods train to fall down embankment.
21 Dec 1955	Cahir, Co Tipperary	2	–	Beet Special crashed through viaduct into River Suir.
23 Dec 1957	Dundrum, Co Dublin	1	4	Suburban railcar train crashed into preceding railcar train.
21 Oct 1974	Gormanston, Co Meath	2	26	Runaway train crashed into two trains at the station.
31 Dec 1975	Clogh, Co Wexford	5	30	Train crashed at underbridge damaged by lorry with high load.
20 Dec 1978	Lisburn, Co Antrim	1	8	*Enterprise* crashed into local train stopped at platform.
3 Oct 1979	Arklow, Co Wicklow	–	30	Train struck by shunting wagons.
16 Nov 1979	Dalkey, Co Dublin	–	36	Commuter train crashed into rear of the preceding commuter train.
1 Aug 1980	Buttevant, Co Cork	18	75	Dublin-Cork express derailed by temporary points in station.
21 Aug 1983	Cherryville, Co Kildare	7	55	Train crashed into crowded rear of train stalled by lack of fuel.
24 Sept 1989	Bekan, Co Mayo	–	80	Knock Pilgrimage Special crashed into cattle herded along rail track.

After the fatal crash through the floor of the Cahir Viaduct, Co Tipperary on 21 December 1955.

| 8 Nov 1997 | Knockcroghery, Co Roscommon | – | 4 | Train derailed by faulty track. |
| 4 June 2002 | Downhill, Co Derry | – | 12 | Train crashed into landslide. |

SELECT BIBLIOGRAPHY

Coogan, Tim Pat, *The Troubles: Ireland's Ordeal 1966-96 and the Search for Peace* (Arrow Books)

Currie, J. L. R., *The Runaway Train: Armagh 1889* (David & Charles, Newtown Abbot, 1971)

Farry, Michael, *The Aftermath of Revolution: Sligo 1921-23* (Benbulben Press, Sligo, 1991)

Fayle, H. and Newham, A., *The Waterford & Tramore Railway* (David & Charles, Newtown Abbot, 1972)

Fitzgerald, Desmond and Weatherup Roger, *The Way We Were* (Friar's Bush Press, Belfast, 1993)

Fryer, C. E. J., *The Waterford & Limerick Railway* (Oakwood Press, Usk, 2000)

Hadden, George, *War on the Railways in Wexford 1922-23* (Irish Railway Record Society, 1953)

Haines, Keith, *Human Frailty and the 1871 Ballymacarrett Rail Accident* (Haines, Belfast, 2002)

Hopkinson, Michael, *Green Against Green: The Irish Civil War* (Gill& Macmillan, Dublin, 2004)

Johnston, Jack, *In the Days of the Clogher Valley* (Friar's Bush Press, Belfast, 1987)

Morton, Grenfell, *Railways in Ulster* (Friar's Bush Press, Belfast, 1989)

Murray, David, *The Straboe Collision 1944* (Irish Railway Record Society Journal, October 1983)

Murray, David, *The Cahir Accident 1955* (Irish Railway Record Society Journal, June 1985)

Murray, Kevin A., *The Great Southern & Western Railway* (Irish Railway Record Society, 1976)

Newham, A. T. and Jenkins, C. J., *The Cork & Muskerry Railway* (Oakwood Press, Headington,1992)

O'Connor, Kevin, *Ironing the Land* (Gill& Macmillan, Dublin, 1999)

O'Meara, John, *The Athenry & Tuam Railway* (Irish Railway Record Society Journal, February 1989)

Patterson, E. M., *A History of the Narrow-Gauge Railways of North East Ireland – Part One* (David & Charles)

Patterson, E. M., *A History of the Narrow-Gauge Railways of North West Ireland – Part Two* (David & Charles)

Patterson, E. M., *The Belfast & County Down Railway* (David & Charles, Newtown Abbot, 1982)

Patterson, E. M., *The Great Northern Railway (Ireland)* (Oakwood Press, Usk, 2003)

Shepherd, Ernie, *The Dublin & South Eastern Railway* (David & Charles, Newtown Abbot, 1974)

Shepherd, Ernie, *The Midland & Great Western Railway of Ireland* (Midland Publ, Leicester, 1994)

Rowlands, David, McGrath, Walter and Francis, Tom, *The Dingle Train* (Plateway Press, Brighton, 1996)

Taylor, Patrick, *The West Clare Railway* (Plateway Press, Brighton, 1994)

Ua Cnáimhsí, *Seantraen Loch Súilí* (Glór Ghaoth Dobhair, Gaoth Dobhair, 1985)

Note: Journals of the Irish Railway Record Society contain accounts of most of the accidents that have occurred on the railways of Ireland since the middle of the nineteenth century.

INDEX OF INCIDENTS